by Sigrid
Cart

On Foot

Circular Walks on Lesvos

Contents

Walks in the Centre and West

Walks in the North-East

Authors' Note

All the routes in this book are described as they were when we last walked them, between December 2010 and February 2012.

While we have taken every care to ensure that our descriptions are complete and accurate, and that the routes we suggest can be completed safely and enjoyably, we can of course accept no responsibility for any difficulties you may encounter while using this book.

Lesvos is a working island, which is one of its many attractions. Visitors, while made very welcome, are of secondary importance to its economy and most of its residents. So when a farmer, as is increasingly the case, decides to enclose his land behind high fences and locked gates, he is unlikely to think of the interests of those of us who would like to walk across it. It's nothing personal!

Change is constant, and in all probability you will find some things which are not as they were when we were writing. Between us we live at least eighteen months of each year on Lesvos, and much of that time is spent walking. Any significant changes that we find are posted on our website, www.lesvoswalks.net, in downloadable and printable form. But we can't be everywhere, so if you find anything that you think should be noted, please send us an email at changes@lesvoswalks.net, or write to the address on the copyright page.

Introduction

About this Book

Until recently most visitors to Lesvos came to the island on one or two week package holidays and stayed in the northern villages of Molivos, Petra or Anaxos. (This is how we both arrived for the first time at different times in the past). For that reason our previous book, 'On Foot in North Lesvos', concentrated almost exclusively on walks starting from one or other of those resorts, and exploring an area between the coast and the Lepetimnos mountain range behind it to the south.

More and more, however, our visitors want to explore further afield, and are hiring their own transport in order do so; not surprising as our adopted island is the third largest and probably most scenically diverse in Greece.

So it was that while Sigrid and I were preparing the fourth edition of 'On Foot in North Lesvos' in 2009 we came to the conclusion that we should widen our, and your, horizons, by providing a selection of walks throughout the island. We gave ourselves a number of rules:- the starting and finishing points of each walk should be within reasonable driving distance of the main resorts: they should as far

as possible be circular, starting and finishing in the same place to avoid the need for more than one vehicle: they should visit places of interest, many of which are inaccessible by car: and last but not least, they should start and finish at or near a friendly taverna or cafenion for a well-deserved after-walk late lunch. (We ourselves have established a tradition, during the preparation of the book, of always rounding off a day's exploration with mezedes and a bottle of retsina!).

Two winters' later, during which, weather permitting (it usually did) we have walked two or three days a week, exploring, eliminating dead ends and false leads, and occasionally getting hopelessly lost (so you don't have to!), this is the result. Hopefully this book does what it says on the cover:- provides a guide to a selection of circular walks around the beautiful and ever-fascinating island of Lesvos. While we have added brief descriptions of the main places and points of interest on each walk, it is not, and does not try to be, a comprehensive guide to the island: for that you will need one of the well-illustrated locally published guide-books, or the relevant sections in one of the many guides to the Greek Islands.

Most of the walks described in this book are completely new, and the result of our own research and exploration, together or separately, either specially for the purposes of this book, or previously during the years that we each have spent here. Throughout, we have done our best not to duplicate routes that have been previously published elsewhere - however, we have not taken this to unreasonable lengths: where we felt that a place was of special interest and had to be included, it was sometimes impossible for us to avoid some of the paths or tracks used by other writers before us who had felt the same way.

So it's now up to you. We hope you will enjoy this book, and make good use of it. And that seeing places, people, and things that you might not otherwise have done will inspire you to return in future years to explore on your own account. Sigrid and I will continue to explore together, and hopefully in a few years time we will have another collection for you to enjoy – the possibilities here are almost inexhaustible; certainly more than enough for my lifetime!

Safe and happy walking!
   Mike Maunder

How to use the book

Please read the following notes before setting off – this should help you get the most out of your walks.

Preparation, Equipment, etc

With a few exceptions, the walks in this book are walks, not 'treks'; most of them easy, or, at most, of medium difficulty. Any exceptions are noted in the introductions to each walk.

They are mainly along well-defined tracks or footpaths, and call for no special clothing or equipment. Long trousers are advisable to protect your legs against the Greek vegetation, which is almost invariably spiny and aggressive, especially once it has dried out during the summer. For your feet, good trainers with solid non-slip soles are quite sufficient. That you take a hat, sun protection and plenty of water should go without saying. A mobile phone can be useful in case of emergency, though you should be aware that signal coverage can be very patchy (and in some places will come via Turkey, making a local phone call for a taxi very expensive!)

Please read through the descriptions of each walk before setting out and judge its length and difficulty against your party's capabilities. The best months for walking are May, early June, September and October; in midsummer, July and August, it can get <u>very</u> hot and shade will be in short supply. Allow time for a slower pace and more rests, take even more water and be aware of the danger of overheating and dehydration. Also the vegetation will be tinder-dry; be especially careful not to start any fires.

We have tried to make the descriptions in this book detailed enough to make maps and other aids superfluous, though we have added GPS co-ordinates at key points for readers who wish to use them. We have given very brief driving directions to the starting point of each walk, but you may find it useful to have a road map with you for reference.

Co-ordinates, Distances and Times

At each significant point you will find bracketed information in the text similar to this:- *[2. 22.74'/11.08', 1.69km/190m, 5 min]*

Reference

*[**2.** 22.74'/11.08', 1.69km/190m, 5 min]* This cross-refers to the point number on the map accompanying each walk.

GPS Co-ordinates

*[2. **22.74'/11.08'**, 1.69km/190m, 5 min]* These are shown as minutes of latitude (N) and longitude (E) to the nearest 1/100th of a minute. (At this latitude 1/100th of a minute is approximately 15 metres.)

They were established on the ground using a handheld Garmin e-Trex receiver (set to WGS 84 map datum), and subsequently double-checked against Google Earth readings.

To save space, we have omitted degrees, except for the first reference in each walk, and in the rare cases where they change along the route.

Distances

*[22.74'/11.08', **1.69km/190m**, 5 m]* These are also taken from e-Trex readings, and are the approximate calculated distances from the starting point of the walk, and from the previous reading.

The approximate total distance for each walk is shown at the beginning of the description.

Note the word 'approximate'. The e-Trex takes satellite readings several times a minute and calculates direction and distance from them. The distance represents horizontal progress, as across a map, not actual metres walked, so will almost always be an under-estimate, especially in hilly areas.

Timings

*[22.74'/11.08', 1.69km/190m, **5 min**]* These are the actual elapsed times, at a reasonably brisk walking pace, from the previous point. They are watch times, and include brief halts to check landmarks, tie shoe-laces, sip water etc, but not longer rest breaks.

It is advisable to try one or two of the shorter walks first, to measure your speed against ours, and make the necessary adjustments before tackling the longer routes.

The approximate total time for each walk is also shown at the beginning of the description.

Definitions

We have tried to be consistent in our use of words, though in some cases, particularly with 'dirt roads' and 'tracks' the distinctions might become blurred, and even change depending on the time of year, weather conditions etc when we wrote the description.

Broadly, therefore:-

Dirt Roads (also **Forest Roads**) are unsurfaced, but compacted and (usually) graded. They are used by all vehicles apart from buses, though taxi drivers are also often reluctant. They are often sign-posted with green finger-posts hand-lettered in white.

Tracks are also wide enough to take vehicles, but are often privately bull-dozed to give access to a particular piece of land or building, left un-compacted, and deteriorate rapidly if unused.

Paths (Monopatia – μονοπάτια and Kalderimia – καλντερίμια) are footpaths, either formal, often walled on either side and running between fields or olive groves, or informal paths across open land or olive groves. The former are often kalderimia, the old cobbled paths between settlements, now in many cases fallen into disrepair.

Gates: Almost all cultivated land in Lesvos is fenced or walled. We have noticed an increasing tendency in the past few years for farmers to block access to their land, and so for this book we have kept to established tracks and footpaths, and only crossed private

land where absolutely unavoidable. However, most gates are still there to keep stock in or mark property boundaries rather than keep people out, and may be used unless padlocked or firmly wired shut. They can be anything from a strand of barbed wire to a wrought-iron creation set between stone pillars; most popular are lengths of concrete reinforcing mesh and old single bed frames (which are just the right size for a gate across a track). You will also find barriers of brushwood piled across gaps to prevent animals from straying. As you would anywhere, always leave them as you find them. While we have noted gates and other barriers which we know to be reasonably permanent, they do frequently come and go, and you may well find ones which we have not.

Farm buildings can range from large modern concrete cattle-sheds through ancient stone byres to sheds pieced together from scrap timber and sheet metal.

River - and stream - beds are usually dry, or carrying only a trickle of water, during the holiday season from May to October. In the wet season, from late October on, or after unseasonable storms, however, they can become torrents or subject to flash floods. While these dates used to be predictable (there were always thunder-storms in the second week of October), climate change seems to be bringing more storms at other times of the year: if you are planning a walk that involves crossing, or walking along, a stream- or river-bed, take extra care in unfavourable weather.

Flora and Fauna

This is not intended to be a wildlife guide, and we have not attempted to identify the plants and animals that you may meet, beyond the obvious trees; oaks, pines, and the ubiquitous olives used as landmarks. Efstathiadis of Athens publishes well- illustrated field guides to wild flowers, trees, birds, etc. in several languages, which are available in local bookshops. There is also 'Wild Flowers of Greece' a comprehensive and beautifully illustrated guide published by Mediterraneo Editions of Crete.

As mentioned previously, Greek vegetation, almost by definition, is aggressive. It has spikes, spines and thorns and will use them on any unprotected flesh, especially at ankle level. Particularly in summer, anything described here as 'pasture' or 'meadow' will consist almost entirely of thorn bushes and thistles. And if those don't get you the holly oak will!

Most wild animals will sense you before you see them, and get out of your way. You may see red squirrels and foxes, and if you are very lucky a pine marten. There are tortoises, terrapins and frogs in ponds and cisterns, and of course lizards of various sizes and colours everywhere.

There is one poisonous snake in Lesvos, the Nose-horned Viper, whose bite is extremely dangerous and often fatal, but it is described as 'slow and rather phlegmatic, not very irascible' and you are unlikely to come across a live one except possibly as a rustling in the undergrowth as you pass. You are much more likely to see the plain brown Montpellier Snake (easily confused with the legless Glass Lizard), or the slim European Cat Snake. Both of these are technically venomous, but as their fangs are at the back of the jaw you are unlikely to be bitten unless you try to stick a finger down their throat!

Lesvos is a paradise for bird-watchers, as it is on spring and autumn migration routes, but if you are a bird-watcher you will know this already and have come prepared.

Dogs, of course, are everywhere. Like their owners, the vast majority of island dogs are friendly: the frantic barking of a tethered dog more often comes from boredom and a wish for attention than from aggressiveness. However it is of course sensible to use normal caution when dealing with them.

It is also worth noting that the majority of dogs you may come across will be working animals, not pets, and are not cosseted as domestic dogs might be in northern Europe. Their owners have hard lives, often for little reward, and so may their dogs. However most are well looked after and there is very little deliberate cruelty.

A note about marked routes

Over the past few years there has been an increased awareness in Lesvos of the number of visitors interested in exploring on foot, and there have been a number of local and EU (Leader) sponsored initiatives to clear and mark walking routes in various parts of the island. Several of our walks use parts of these routes, and you may well come across waymarks and finger-posts along the way. Unfortunately, budgets for their maintenance are scanty or non-existent, and many of the signs are already collapsing or becoming illegible. As we have no way of knowing what their condition when you come to use this book, we have not used them in our descriptions.

Useful Information

Local Transport

Buses

The country bus service across Lesvos is sparse, and it is unrealistic to try to use buses instead of your own vehicle for any of these walks.

In general there is an early morning bus from the main outlying towns into Mitilini, and an early afternoon one back, with possibly one or two additional services during the rest of the day to resorts. Local tourist information offices will usually have an up-to-date timetable, which may also be posted at the main bus stop in your resort.

Taxis

As everywhere in Greece, taxis are plentiful and convenient. There are taxi stands in the main resorts, as well as Mitilini and Kalloni, and many villages have their own taxis. It is useful to note the phone number of a local taxi or taxi stand where you are staying, for use in emergency!

Emergency Phone Numbers

Police, Ambulance etc: 112

Fire: 199

The Skalas & Kampos of Lesvos

Most of the original settlements in Lesvos were on or near the coast, to take advantage of easy access to the sea for fishing and transport, as well as the the fertile and easily cultivated soil of the coastal plains. Divided into small farms and small-holdings, and close to the villages where farmers returned home each day, these areas were and still are known as 'ο κάμπος', literally 'the plain'.

From the middle ages on, however, the increasing frequency of pirate raids from the sea forced the inhabitants to retreat inland, either to more easily defended hill villages such as Sikaminias, or to sites hidden from the sea like Vrisa and Eresos.

They retained their all-important access to the sea at their Skala (Σκάλα), literally a ladder or staircase, where the fishermen of the village could moor their boats and clean their nets. Over the centuries, as the threats decreased, people came to spend more time at the skala rather than walk the several kilometres to and fro from their villages each day, and gradually they once again became permanent settlements, though even today their inhabitants usually retain strong links with their 'parent' villages.

Secret Bays – Skala Loutron
& Agios Ermogenis

Total distance 10½ kilometres

 Walking time 3½ hours

The Gulf of Gera is one of our favourite parts of Lesvos. Remote from most foreign tourism, it has plentiful unspoiled bays and simple tavernas known only to the locals. This walk takes you through some of the most beautiful parts of the eastern side of the gulf (Walk 15 - Along the Gulf of Gera from Avlonas to Katsinia shows you some of the west) It alternates between beaches, olive groves, and pine forest, with the opportunity for a swim and lunch at the halfway point. There are summer tavernas at the harbour in Skala Loutron and on the beach at Agios Ermogenis._

The route follows a figure of eight route totalling 10½km, but you have the option of shorter walks starting at either Skala Loutron (5¾km) or Agios Ermogenis (3½km) and completing one circle of the eight. The variations are given in the descriptions below.

Start from the parking area by the fishing harbour in Skala Loutron *[1. 39°02.71'/26°31.90']*. Turn right along the road past the boatyard and continue uphill on the concrete street through the village.

At the far side, where the concrete ends and the dirt road bends slightly left, go right through a wide gateway on to a field track *[2. 02.42'/31.98', 560m, 10 min]*. Follow it downhill through an olive grove, and then past fenced plots. The track turns sharp right at gates, passes a chapel on the left, and ends at the sea-shore *[3. 02.34'/31.68', 1.11km/550m, 10 min]*.

Turn left along the beach, then go slightly left up through a gate on to a path *[4. 02.29'/31.58', 1.29km/180m, 3 min]*. Follow the path along above the shore-line: when it becomes faint return to the beach and cross rocks around a small bay (take care here, the rocks can be slippery and at high water you may get wet feet!) *[5. 02.34'/31.29', 1.80km/510m, 12 min]*.

At the end of the bay return to a small path and continue parallel with the shore until the way is blocked by a fence *[6. 02.29'/31.27', 1.95km/150m, 8 min]*. Go round the end of the fence on rocks above the shore, and immediately back on to a path along the top of the sea wall.

The path continues along the shore. It is joined by a field track coming in from the left, which after about 100 metres veers left before rejoining the path 50 metres later. The track soon ends, leaving the path to bend left uphill, up a steep bank at the right-hand end of a low cliff, and on up for a few metres to a gap in a fence (you may find a gate or brushwood barrier here) *[7. 02.05'/31.46', 2.55km/600m, 12 min]*.

Go through and continue parallel to the sea. Ignore a small path off to the left after about 60 metres, but stay on the main path, which leads slightly to the left and gently uphill until it approaches a dense bramble thicket. It then goes diagonally left up a bank to a terrace wall, bends to the right, continues to a partly ruined farmhouse *[8. 01.88'/31.54', 2.92km/370m, 7 min]*.

From the farmhouse a track leads on downhill. It reaches a gate and levels out *[9. 01.74'/31.77', 3.36km/440m, 8 min]*. It goes on through another gate, by farm buildings, and then a third *[10. 01.76'/31.93', 3.61km/250m, 7 min]*. Just offshore to the right

you will see the cages of the nearby fish farm.

Continue to a T-junction and turn right *[11. 01.76'/32.03', 3.75km/140m, 3 min].* **(For the shorter walk from Skala Loutron, turn left here and continue from point 20 below)** Go along the dirt road past fish farm buildings and holding tanks, then uphill. At the brow of the hill there are further large fish farm buildings and tanks to the left and right. Carry on along the road, ignoring side tracks, and passing another large building above on the right, until you come to an offset crossing, with a track coming in from the left, and then one going off to the right *[12. 01.53'/32.66', 5.05km/1.30km, 20 min].*

Take the field track to the right and walk through the olive grove until you arrive at an asphalt road *[13. 01.30'/32.77', 5.60km/550m, 6 min].* Turn right on to the road and walk uphill, with orchards below you to the left. When the road bends right to reveal the sea below ignore the tracks leading invitingly off to the left, but continue on the road until you reach a concrete path on the left with a hand-painted fingerpost to ΑΓΙΟ ΕΡΜΟΓΕΝΗC *[14. 01.05'/32.61', 6.25km/650m, 15 min].* Go down the path until you reach a small group of white and blue painted buildings. The chapel of Ag Ermogenis is on the cliff edge down the steps to the left. A shaded terrace overlooks the beautiful bay, while behind the chapel a long flight of steps leads down to the next beach *[15. 01.01'/32.60', 6.37km/120m, 3 min].*

Go on down the paved path to the beach for a swim, lunch at the beach taverna, or both. To resume your walk go up the concrete road behind the taverna (distances and timings continue from point 15) and round the first right-hand bend on to asphalt. At the next bend take the path on the left leading straight up the hillside into the pine forest *[16. 01.00'/32.48', 6.63km/260m, 5 min].*

Follow the path to the brow of the hill, and then down the other side towards the sea. Where it divides on the downhill stretch keep to the right. Caution: parts of this stretch, both up- and downhill are very steep, with a loose, stony surface. Be very careful.

When you reach the beach carry on through the olive grove with the sea on your left, passing a cement-block barn on your right, to arrive at a gate *[17. 01.14'/32.29', 6.97km/340m, 15 min].* Go to the right along the beach for about 100 metres, then veer right up a path behind the beach, follow it back down to the beach, then almost immediately back on to a path.

Follow this until it joins the end of a track *[18. 01.39'/32.12', 7.53km/560m, 12 min]*. Continue on the track, keeping right where it forks on an uphill bend. It passes a stone-built cistern on the left, then turns sharp left at high metal gates into an olive grove, and ends at a T-junction *[19. 01.54'/32.28', 7.94km/410m, 8 min]*. **(For the shorter walk from Agios Ermogenis, turn right here for about 600m and continue from point 12 above)**

Turn left on to the dirt road (this was part of your outward route) and follow it back past the fish farms to the junction at point 11 *[20. 01.76'/32.03', 8.65km/710m, 10 min]*. Now go straight ahead, ignoring side tracks: the track hairpins uphill before leading back to Skala Loutron. Return through the village, retracing your outward route, to reach the harbour-side car park. *[21. 02.71'/31.90', 10.66km/2.01km, 35 min]*.

A Forest Walk from Akrotiri to Panagia Amalis

2

Total distance 8½ kilometres

 Walking time 3¼ hours

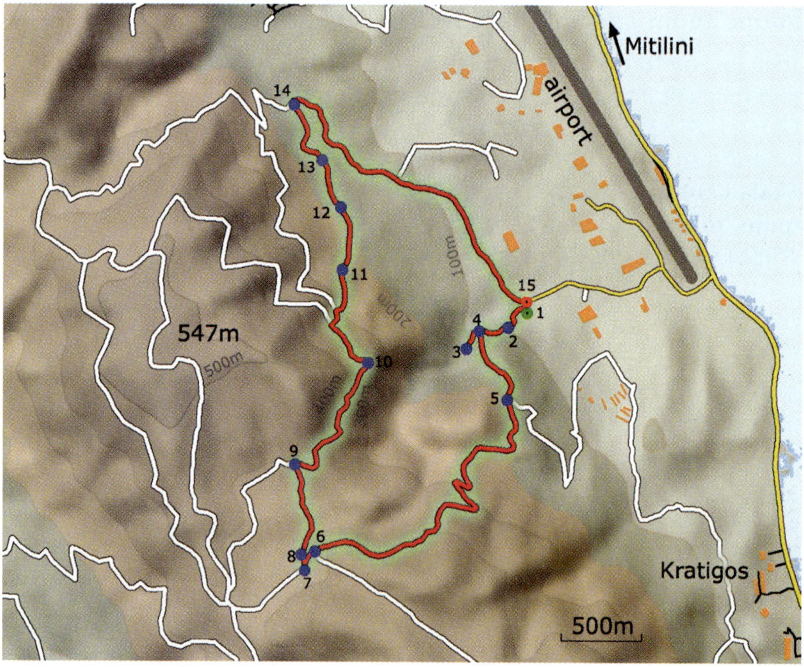

This walk starts less than a kilometre from the runway of Mitilini airport, but you will probably meet nobody throughout the whole 8½ kilometres. The airport is sandwiched between the sea and a range of low, pine-forest clad mountains which run south from Mitilini and rise to 547m at their highest point a mere 3km from the airport terminal. Our walk only reaches 375m, at the church and picnic spot of Panagia Amalis, but involves some steep climbs and descents, sometimes on loose and stony paths.

The starting point is at the foot of the Kratigos Gorge (Λαγκάδα Κρατήγου), a deep ravine leading into the mountain, lined with the ruins of old water mills, ten in all, which once operated throughout the year: what is now a beautiful and isolated spot would then have been a hive of activity. To get here continue south along the coast road from Mitilini past the airport until you reach the end of the high perimeter fence. Almost immediately, take the turning to the right, and follow the road as it swings right back round the edge of the airport. At the next junction turn left and follow the road inland past an army base on the left and the ruins of an Ottoman aqueduct on the right. After about a kilometre it bends right into the forest past another section of masonry aqueduct. Park here on the wide entrance to a track on the left of the bend.

This is your starting point *[1. 39°02.83'/26°35.63']*. Walk along the track, which almost immediately forks. Take the left-hand path down to, and across a river-bed, then go right on to a small footpath *[2. 02.78'/35.59', 130m, 2 min]*. It leads under the arch of a mill water-course, then up to a T-junction. Keep right here, and continue above the ravine past more mill remains and a modern pump-house (the springs which once drove the mills are now piped into Mitilini's water supply). Ignore a path leading down to the stream on your right, and (for the moment) two small paths going uphill on the left. Continue on the level path (there are faded yellow

diamond waymarks along this stretch) until it ends at a wide stone pavement which continues up the valley for about 200 metres *[3. 02.72'/35.42', 430m/300m, 15 min]*.

This was once the river-bed, which was paved to help control the flow of water to the mills – most of the water is now piped beneath the paving and emerges below the weir on your right.

Retrace your steps for 60 metres to the foot of a small path leading uphill (the first few metres look like a rocky stream bed) *[4. 02.75'/35.43', 490m/60m, 2 min]*. Turn right up this, and follow it steeply uphill through the forest along the edge of a smaller valley. Finally, after an even steeper few metres, it emerges on to a track *[5. 02.55'/35.56', 945m/455m, 15 min]*.

Turn right on to the track, and continue uphill. Climb up through hairpin bends, with alternating views down to the sea, the airport, Mitilini, Turkey, and across the valley to the forests and mountain peaks beyond. Finally the track levels out and even runs gently downhill. Continue ahead where a wide track forks off to the left *[6. 02.07'/34.78', 3.17km/2.22km, 40 min]* and go round a gentle left-hand bend to reach Panagia Amalis (Παναγία Αμαλής) – the Madonna of Amalis. There is a small, modern, well-kept church here, a wide picnic areas with tables and benches, and a covered pavilion under the trees for hotter days *[7. 01.99'/34.73', 3.35km/180m, 3 min]*.

After your break, go back along the track for about 100 metres

(there may be an information board here), and take the footpath running diagonally left into the forest *[8. 02.01'/34.72', 3.40km/50m, 1 min]*. The next 3 kilometres is part of a hiking route from Agia Marina to Panagia Amalis, and is copiously marked with finger-posts, yellow trekking-trail signs, and red diamond waymarks. There are also picnic benches and rubbish bins in several places along the way.

When the path rises to cross a track and continue uphill, turn right on to the track *[9. 02.33'/34.68', 4.02km/620m, 13 min]* and follow it as it winds along the edge of a deep valley. Finally, at a sharp left-hand bend, where there may be a finger-post and information board *[10. 02.63'/34.97', 4.87km/850m, 16 min]* a footpath leads ahead to a viewing point high above the sea. This is Provasma (Πρόβασμα), and the highest point of the walk.

From the viewpoint go down to the left on a steep, stony path. It rises briefly back towards the track – ignore a short path up to the left which rejoins the track after a few metres. Much of this next stretch is both steep and loose, and demands great care. Eventually the path crosses a plank bridge and swings right *[11. 02.96'/34.90', 5.53km/660m, 30 min]*.

Continue, crossing a group of three plank bridges *[12. 03.15'/34.85', 5.88km/350m, 10 min]*, until the path forks *[13. 03.29'/34.79', 6.13km/250m, 7 min]*. Keep ahead on the upper path. (Ignore a finger-post pointing down right to ΑΓ ΜΑΡΙΝΑ – the path runs parallel to but below the main one, and rejoins it at the top of the next climb.)

Continue on the main path until it ends at a T-junction with a track *[14. 03.46'/34.67', 6.55km/420m, 5 min]*. Turn right, and immediately right again on to a dirt road. Continue on this, ignoring side roads to the left. It eventually becomes asphalt, and soon afterwards reaches your starting point *[15. 02.83'/35.63', 8.61km/2.06km, 30 min]*.

Just before it does, on the left alongside the water-course, two large plastic greenhouse-like structures house a breeding centre for the Chukar (Alectoris chukar)- local name Νησιωτική Πέρδικα, Island Partridge – with the aim of re-introducing it into the wild. For Greek readers, a sign at the entrance gives more details and forbids entrance!

To the Roman Aqueduct of Moria

3

Total distance 8¾ kilometres

Walking time 2¾ hours

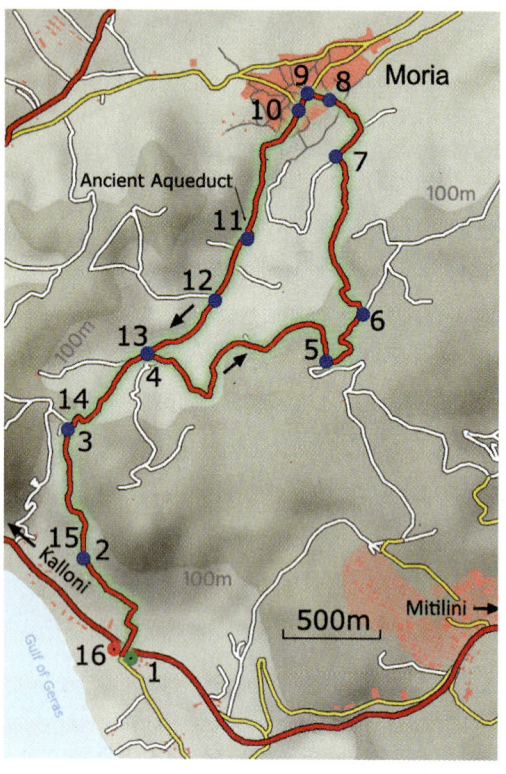

The remains of the Roman aqueduct at Moria are among the most impressive archaeological sites of Lesvos. It was originally thought to have been built during the reign of the emperor Hadrian in the 2nd or 3rd century AD (it is intriguing to speculate that the same civil engineers, working in a back office in Rome, might also have drawn up plans for Hadrian's Wall), but more recent opinion dates it to the 1st century BC during the reign of Agrippa, himself an engineer, who spent long periods in Mitilini between 23 and 13BC.

The aqueduct supplied approximately 127,000 cubic meters of fresh water per day to Mitilini from the springs of mount Olympos near Agiasos. It is believed that it began below Olympos at Megali Limni (Μεγάλη Λίμνη), the large lake, now drained, at the foot of Olympos, and took the water for 26 kilometres on a convoluted route to Mitilini, following the contours of the land to ensure a constant gentle gradient. The seventeen arches (kamares, καμάρες) here, the largest surviving section of the aqueduct, were built largely of local grey marble, and have been the object of extensive conservation and restoration work over the last decade. (To visit a shorter but almost as impressive section, take walk 6 from Karini to Paspala.)

This walk takes you from the edge of the Gulf of Gera through a hilly landscape of olive groves to the old chapel of Our Lady of Outza (Παναγία Ουτζάς), and then through the village street of Moria, before continuing to the aqueduct. It begins and ends next to the Silver Bay Hotel, near Kedro, which is on the Gulf of Gera about five kilometres from Mitilini on the main road to Kalloni. Turn off the main road at the hotel and park in the lane alongside.

From the starting point [1. 39°06.48'/26°30.43'], cross the main road with care and take the rough track leading uphill directly opposite. It soon bends left to follow the upper boundary of a fenced olive grove, above and parallel with the main road and the gulf. Where the fence ends continue on the path leading up through

terraces of olive trees, until it reaches a small level area at the end of another track. *[2. 06.73'/30.29', 660m, 13 min]*.

Bear right on to the track as it leads up through the olive groves, with views down through the valley on the left back to the gulf. It levels out, then descends to a T-junction. *[3. 07.07'/30.24', 1.33km/670m, 14 min]*. Turn right and follow the track as it winds downhill, passing a spring and stone trough (dated 1974) on the right. Ignore a minor track coming in diagonally from the left, and continue to a junction to the right, signposted ΠΡΟΣ ΠΑΝΑΓΙΑ ΟΥΤΖΑ. *[4. 07.26'/30.52', 1.90km/570m, 12 min]*.

Take this turning, and keep left after a few metres at the next junction. To the left you will soon get your first view of the aqueduct. Continue uphill on concrete to the next junction, and take the track leading downhill to the left, again signposted ΠΡΟΣ ΠΑΝΑΓΙΑ ΟΥΤΖΑ. *[5. 07.24'/31.12', 3.26km/1.36km, 25 min]*. There are views of the village of Moria ahead, and you will shortly arrive at the short track leading to the chapel of Παναγία Ούτζα (Our Lady of Outza). *[6. 07.37'/31.25', 3.66km/400m, 6 min]*. The chapel is relatively modern, but appears to be built on ancient foundations (there is archaeological evidence of ancient settlements in this area), and is a pleasant spot for a break.

Then take the path leading downhill to the right from the front of the chapel. It runs through an olive grove, with a small valley to the right. Follow it down into the valley, across a stream, and continue down, with the valley now on your left. Take care; the path is rough, rocky, and steep in places. It arrives at a fenced olive grove and turns left along the boundary to arrive at a T-junction with a level track. *[7. 07.78'/31.16', 4.61km/950m, 25 min]*.

Turn right, and at the next junction keep left. Cross a concrete bridge into the outskirts of Moria (you will see the local football ground a short distance away to your right.) At the next junction *[8. 07.93'/31.14', 5.00km/390m, 6 min]* keep left straight up the street ahead into the centre. At the junction with the main street, lined with small shops and kafenions, turn left *[9. 07.95'/31.07', 5.11km/110m, 3 min]*.

Walk along the main street until it bends right. Keep left, and follow the street ahead. There is an inconspicuous sign on the wall facing you at this point - 'ΠΡΟΣ ΑΡΧΑΙΟΝ ΥΔΡΑΓΩΓΕΙΟΝ – ΤΟ ΤΗΕ

ANCIENT AQUEDUCT' *[10. 07.92'/31.03', 5.18km/70m, 2 min].* Follow the paved street straight ahead out of the village (there is another sign pointing ahead where a potentially misleading street goes off to the left) and continue through the wide valley until you come to the aqueduct *[11. 07.57'/30.87', 5.95km/770m, 11 min].*

After exploring the aqueduct and its surroundings carry on along the dirt road away from Moria, ignoring side tracks to right and left, until you reach a more prominent junction by a concrete hut and large electricity pole *[12. 07.41'/30.75', 6.30km/350m, 8 min].* Continue ahead on the left-hand road until you reach a junction to the left signposted ΠΡΟΣ ΠΑΝΑΓΙΑ ΟΥΤΖΑ. *[13. 07.26'/30.52', 6.75km/450m, 8 min].* This was point 4 on the outward route and from here you retrace your steps to return to the starting point.

So carry straight on at this junction, keep left at the next fork, following the sign 'ΠΡΟΣ ΑΓΙΟ ΡΑΦΑΗΛ' (St Raphael), and then left again after climbing the hill past the spring. *[14. 07.07'/30.24', 7.33km/580m, 9 min].* (The track ahead continues up, signposted to ΠΡΟΦ ΗΛΙΑ – Profitis Ilias, the local high point). Continue to the end of the track, with the Gulf of Gera now lying ahead of you down to the right. When the track ends, *[15. 06.73'/30.29', 8.02km/690m, 10 min]* go steeply downhill through the terraces and along the fenced olive grove to reach the main road and your starting point *[16. 06.48'/30.43', 8.68km/660m, 15 min].*

A Circular Walk from Skala Neon Kidonion

4

Total distance 8½ kilometres

 Walking time 3 hours

The east coast of Lesvos north of Mitilini is hardly known to foreign tourists, though many Greeks come from the mainland to holiday in the small resorts here during July and August. One of these is Skala Neon Kidonion, a small fishing village whose harbour is sheltered by a headland, on which there is a large taverna.

The area has a chequered history: the original settlement of Kidonies (Κυδωνιές) was on the plateau to the south of the Skala, known as Plati, where the ruins of a medieval castle lie over traces of a bronze age fortress. When it was destroyed by a massive earthquake in about 1600AD, the surviving inhabitants fled across the sea to the coast of Asia Minor, which was at that time extensively colonised by Greeks from Lesvos, and set up a new town of Kidonies, which is now the Turkish port of Ayvalik (both names mean 'quince orchard' in their respective languages). Three hundred years later, in the exchange of populations that followed the Treaty of Lausanne in 1922, their descendants returned to Lesvos, occupied the former Ottoman village of Baltzik, and renamed it Nees Kidonies (Νέες Κυδωνιές), New Kidonies. The former mosque was converted into the Orthodox church of St George of Chios (and the old church of St George in Ayvalik is now the Çınarlı Mosque).

This walk starts in the Skala, and takes you through orchards and up a well-preserved kalderimi to the 'mother village' of Nees Kidonies. From there you descend through olive groves into a green valley, and climb again to Plati, where you can explore the castle ruins before returning down a beautiful footpath to the Skala.

Skala Neon Kidonion is close to the main coast road from Mitilini to Mantamados, mid-way (about 17km in each direction) between the two. Look for the signs, then follow the road down to the sea, and turn right along the shore to the end of the harbour.

Park at the foot of the headland beyond the harbour. The walk starts and finishes here. *[1. 39°14.01'/26°27.28']*

Walk along the beach road away from the village. Shortly before the asphalt surface comes to an end turn right up an asphalt lane alongside a group of modern houses *[2. 13.88'/27.40', 315m, 4 min]*. (The unsurfaced beach road continues for a few metres and ends at a stream crossing the beach).

The lane soon becomes a track between fenced fields, with large greenhouses beyond on the left. When it ends continue ahead into a small field and go straight across it to join a path. Pass a stand of bamboo on your left, and then large greenhouses and a citrus grove on the right. The path ends at a concrete ramp which climbs to join the Mitilini - Mantamados main road *[3. 13.77'/27.06', 895m/580m, 10 min]*.

Turn right and follow the road for 200 metres. Look for a concrete path leading up to the left opposite the road-sign to Skala Neon Kydonion *[4. 13.89'/27.01', 1.13km/235m, 4 min]*. The path leads up to a house gate, and then continues as kalderimi. When you come to a T-junction turn right uphill, still on kalderimi *[5. 13.77'/26.93', 1.37km/240m, 7 min]*, and follow it until you reach an open plateau. *[6. 13.76'/26.86', 1.54km/170m, 7 min]*. Ahead of you there is a fenced quarry containing stacks of enormous rocks, the raw materials for the stone-cutting works to the left.

Turn left uphill, passing the factory, and join its concrete access road to head towards the village of Nees Kydonies, which is visible ahead. When the road bends right past an olive press bear left on to a path alongside a barn *[7. 13.68'/26.66', 1.88km/340m, 7 min]*. Follow this path, ignoring a crossing path, and join a concrete street on the edge of the village. At the first junction take the left-hand street (not the path leading off left at right angles) *[8. 13.55'/26.48', 2.27km/390m, 8 min]*. Turn left at the next T-junction, then right on to a broad kalderimi. Where this bends right *[9. 13.51'/26.43', 2.36km/90m, 3 min]* go to the left across a patch of waste ground and follow a narrow path past a cistern round to the right, with the edge of the village to the right and a precipitous drop into the valley below on the left.

The path joins a dirt road leading downhill out of the village

[10. 13.49'/26.31', 2.57km/210m, 9 min]. Follow it to the left, and stay with it when it hairpins down to the left, ignoring the track leading ahead *[11. 13.45'/26.19', 2.76km/190m, 3 min].* Continue down into the valley on a stretch of concrete. Ignore a lesser track leading ahead at a right-hand hairpin just before the concrete ends, and further side tracks.

In the valley, cross two streams on concrete bridges *[12. 13.18'/26.09', 3.69km/930m, 15 min],* and climb gently up the other side parallel with the stream below. At the next junction take the concrete track leading downhill to the left back into the valley *[13. 13.21'/26.27', 3.95km/260m, 7 min].* Cross a stream-bed and climb again on kalderimi. The track levels out for a short distance, then drops down again to another stream-bed at a junction *[14. 13.24'/26.60', 4.53km/580m, 10 min].*

Keep right, and continue to rise and fall through olive groves until a final steep climb brings you to an oblique T-junction *[15. 13.13'/26.93', 5.08/550m, 11 min].* Go left, and stay on this track, ignoring side tracks, until it rises to meet the Mitilini - Mantamados main road *[16. 12.97'/27.35', 5.78km/700m, 7 min] .*

Cross the road with great care (the road at this point has a

combination of sharp bends and a blind hill-brow – drivers will not be expecting the added complication of crossing pedestrians!), and take the lane leading uphill directly opposite. Follow it until it reaches a wide, flat, plateau *[17. 13.04'/27.45', 5.98km/200m, 4 min]*. Further ahead it is dotted with quarries, but here the main visible features are the ruins of an old stone watch-tower a few hundred metres diagonally to the right, and the long, straight, wide white track which is the racecourse belonging to the Mystegna equestrian society.

Turn left on to this, and follow it to the far end (there may be a set of starting stalls rusting gently here). Then continue along the track between farms and past a charcoal burner's site *[18. 13.49'/27.33', 6.86km/880m, 20 min]*. The track then winds on towards another farm. Just before you reach it a turning through a gate to the left *[19. 13.59'/27.39', 7.09km/230m, 3 min]* leads to the remains of the ancient castle and settlement of Kidonies. (Follow the lane about 200m to an olive grove. The ruins are to the left, in the next olive grove - through a gap in the wall next to the chapel. This diversion is not included in the distances and timings).

Continue on the track past the farm, then follow it as it swings right alongside an enclosure *[20. 13.59'/27.49', 7.25km/160m, 4 min]*. It then bends downhill to the left past another gated charcoal-burning site *[21. 13.58'/26.45', 7.34km/90m, 3 min]*.

Look for a small path diagonally to the left. This leads along to a wall, turns right, then immediately left through a gate *[22. 13.62'/27.54', 7.45km/110m, 5 min]*. It then winds downhill, over rocks, and onto a kalderimi, steep in places, and finally emerges on a steep grassy slope above the sea. Stay on the path until it levels out and leads parallel to the sea along the top edge of a fenced field.

Go to the right through a gap in the fence *[23. 13.79'/27.43', 7.86km/410m, 15 min]*, then diagonally down through the field to the bottom left-hand corner (there several fences, but with gaps left to allow access). Go through the wire-netting gate in the extreme left-hand corner of the final fence on to the beach *[24. 13.84'/27.45', 7.98km/120m, 5 min]*, turn left across a stream, and join the Skala Neon Kydonion beach road to return to your starting point *[25. 14.01'/27.28', 8.38km/400m, 8 min]*.

A City Walk through Mitilini

5

Total distance 5½ kilometres

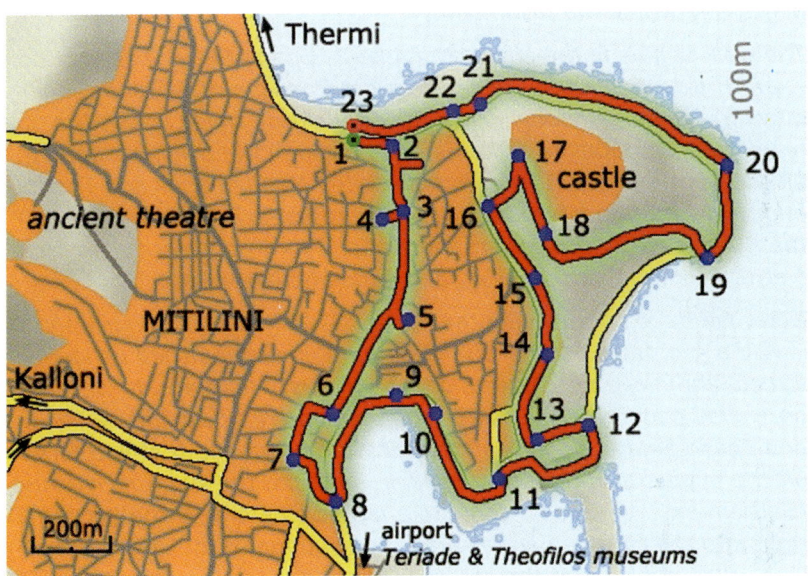

Mitilini's history goes back to the earliest days of Lesvos, when it was one of the six city states sharing the island. It was in turn under ancient Greek, Roman, Byzantine, Genoese and finally Ottoman rule, until in November 1912, with the defeat and expulsion of the Turkish occupiers by Greek and local forces, it became part of the young modern Greek state. Its chequered heritage, however, is still apparent everywhere you go.

Today it is an attractive port city, the busy administrative, business and cultural centre of the island, with a population of approximately 27,000 at the 2001 census (about a third of the total population of the island). It is also the seat of government of the administrative region of the North Aegean and home of its university.

19

This walk takes you to some of the most interesting historical places in the city, as well as giving a taste of its present-day life. We have added some illustrated details of some of the most interesting sites at the end of the walk description. It is a compact city; the distance covered is less than 5½km, barely an hour's brisk walking. However we have not included timings; we hope you will be stopping at unpredictable points along your way, whether at points of interest that we mention, or for coffee, a snack, shopping, or just to sit on a bench and watch the world go by.

The walk begins in the old north harbour, Epano Skala (Επάνω Σκάλα). It is most easily reached by car from the coast road running down from Mandamados, or via the city bypass which leaves the main road from Kalloni as it descends through the trading estates on the city outskirts. Turn left, signposted Mandamados and Thermi, and follow the road over the hill to emerge at a T-junction next to the island's electricity-generating station. Turn right until you reach a stretch of dual-carriageway, and park where you can.

Note: we have not included the ancient Greek theatre in our walk; it is half a kilometre up a steep hill through undistinguished residential streets and has unpredictable opening hours. There are, however, unrivalled panoramic views from its parking area over the castle and Epano Skala. If you wish to visit we recommend that you turn off the bypass at the brow of the hill, following the sign to 'Mytilini (Settlement)'. When you come to a large cemetery on the left, turn right into the theatre parking area. To continue to the start of the walk, turn right out of the car-park, then immediately left alongside

the cemetery and follow the road round to the right. Then continue straight down-hill (take care at the frequent junctions – cross-traffic has priority) until you reach the coast road at the beginning of the dual-carriageway. Turn right and park.

Other places you might like to include in your visit are the Roman aqueduct at Moria, a short distance north of Mitilini, (see Walk 3), and the Theofilos and Teriade Museums at Vareia, in the southern suburbs off the main road to the airport.

Before starting your walk, look out across the water: you will see the remains of two ancient breakwaters which once protected the large harbour here.

The walk starts at the large railed-off archaeological site, the Hellenistic Loggia (or Stoa) immediately to the right of a large white building (a local hospital) *[1. 39°06.72'/26°33.37']*. Walk along in front of the hospital, past masonry from the ancient port and a small chapel, and take the street to the right *[2. 06.72'/33.44', 90m]*. The creeper-covered building on the corner opposite, now a horticultural supplier, was once Yali Camii mosque.

Take the first left and go up the street for a few metres. On the right there is another archaeological site, with remains ranging from Hellenistic period workshops to a late Roman building, perhaps a tavern/brothel, constructed around a colonnaded courtyard. In its final phase the site housed an Ottoman cemetery – the excavators discovered the remains of a middle aged man with 20 cm. spikes through his neck, middle and ankles, apparently buried as a vampire!

Return to the junction and bear round to the left. This is Ermou (Ερμού), the main shopping street of both the old and modern city, which despite being 'improved' and smartened in recent years still retains much of the atmosphere of a bazaar. The street was originally a canal connecting Epano Skala with the bay to the south which is now the modern harbour, and making an island of the high promontory with the castle. Walk along until you come to the large, roofless building behind a railed courtyard on the left. This is the largest and latest surviving mosque, Yeni Camii (New Mosque), built in 1825 *[3. 06.63'/33.46', 290m/200m]*.

Now turn off Ermou to the right, directly opposite Yeni Camii, and walk along to Tarsi Hamam, the restored Ottoman bath-house *[4. 06.62'/33.44', 326m/36m]*. Return to Ermou and continue along to the right until the street forks. Take the left fork for a few metres to the entrance to the Cathedral of St Athanasios (Αγ Αθανάσιος) *[5. 06.50'/33.45', 560m/234m]*.

Go through the precinct to the rear of the cathedral to see the excavated remains of an impressive late-Roman building in marble, possibly the assembly or senate-house of the city.

From the cathedral, return to the junction and continue to the left along Ermou for 300 metres. Take the street to the right opposite the National Bank of Greece *[6. 06.37'/33.34', 877m/317m]*, and walk up to the next junction. Turn left, go straight over at the next crossing, and arrive in the large paved square of St Therapon (Αγ θεράπων) *[7. 06.30'/33.27', 1.07km/193m]*. Opposite the church, on the right-hand side of the square, is the Ecclesiastical Byzantine Museum, with a collection of icons and other Christian art from the 13th to 20th centuries.

Go down the steps at the end of the square and turn left for a few metres to return to Ermou. Turn right. When you come to the junction at the end of the paved street cross and go ahead along the path through a coffee-house. Across to your right beyond the taxi-rank is the impressive neo-classical Experimental Lyceum of Mitilini. Previously the Gymnasium of Mitilini, it was built in 1888-90 to replace the original Gymnasium, which dated from 1840 and was the first Greek school on Lesvos to be authorised by the Ottoman authorities.

Bear left through the gardens to the harbour-side road

[8. 06.25'/33.34', 1.25km/180m]. The large modern building to your right is the Municipal Theatre.

Now cross the road and head left. On the corner of the street directly opposite is the old Town Hall (ΔΗΜΑΡΧΕΙΟ), built in the early years of the 20th century. Walk along the side of the inner harbour – behind you to the right you will see small fishing boats moored alongside the quayside tavernas, but alongside the road here there are usually fast navy and coastguard patrol boats, then, during the fishing season, larger fishing boats, where if you arrive at the right time you can sometimes buy fresh fish from the day's catch straight from the deck. The port tug is also usually moored here.

The quay bends to the right: across the road in a small square you will see a marble bust of the classical poetess Sappho (Σαπφώ), who was a native of the island *[9. 06.39'/33.45', 1.63km/380m].*

The quay turns sharp right again. This is the mooring area for visiting yachts of all shapes and sizes, although a new marina has been built to the south of the harbour. Here you can see another minor relic of the Ottoman empire: across the road, above the awning of a coffee-house, the building still bears the faded sign of its original occupier, the BANQUE IMPERIALE OTTOMANE *[10. 06.37'/33.50', 1.71km/80m].*

Continue along the quayside. Looking across the harbour you will see coastal tankers and bulk carriers unloading in the cargo port beyond the inner breakwater. At the next

23

bend you reach the first entrance gate to the ferry port (there is a large sign ΕΠΙΒΑΤΙΚΟ ΛΙΜΑΝΙ ΜΥΤΙΛΗΝΗΣ). Follow the road round to the left, and then turn right into the port through gate B. *[11. 06.28'/33.62', 2.06km/350m]*. Pass the building on your right, which houses customs and port police, and go ahead towards the car park. Above the domed building ahead (the municipal swimming pool) you will see the Statue of Liberty – this is not a hallucination! At the car park go right back to the quayside, where there will probably be one or two ferries waiting to load for the crossing to the mainland. Go to the left and follow the road round and out of the port. You will find the Statue of Liberty at the T-junction ahead. *[12. 06.35'/33.77', 2.44km/380m]*.

Turn left and walk along towards the next junction. On your right you will see two mansions, typical of those built by Lesvos merchants during the prosperous nineteenth century. The second of these, on the corner site, now houses the 'old' Archaeological Museum *[13. 06.33'/33.68', 2.59km/150m]*.

Turn right up the street next to the museum. **Caution – this is the main exit from the city going north, a narrow, busy, one-way street with very narrow footpaths and traffic coming from behind you. Be extremely careful and alert.** At the top of the street bear right and continue uphill to the modern buildings of the 'new' Museum *[14. 06.44'/33.70', 2.87km/280m]*.

Go on up the road. After nearly 200 metres you come to a paved road to the right which leads up to Mitilini Castle (look for the signboard at the junction) *[15. 06.54'/33.68', 3.08km/210m]*. Continue along the main road; on the brow of the hill you pass the neo-classical Ministry of the Aegean on your right, built in 1893 to house the Ottoman government of the province. Across the road on the left are the Law Courts, originally built in 1895 as the Ottoman High School.

Continue downhill and take the first turning on the right *[16. 06.63'/33.60', 3.29km/210m]*. Go up the concrete street, and when it ends at a school entrance, carry on uphill to the left on to a cobbled road leading to the castle entrance *[17. 06.70'/33.65', 3.44km/150m]*.

(If, after your visit to the castle, you are tired or short of time, and wish to curtail the walk, you can follow the cobbled road down back to the main road. Turn right and follow the main road down to the old harbour, round to the left and in 200 metres you will have returned to your starting point)

Otherwise, on leaving the castle, take the gravel footpath up shallow steps to the left as the entrance road bears right. Follow the path through pine trees alongside the castle's outer wall, and down steps to a paved area (measurements continue from the castle entrance) *[18. 06.60'/33.70', 3.64km/200m].* Cross a small parking area and turn right down the paved road. Then turn left through the car park, and at the far end take the footpath into the pine forest. (You are heading for the road at the foot of the hill which leads round the castle headland. There are several ways of reaching it – this is our suggestion.) Keep right when the path forks and then right again. Turn left at the next two T-junctions, and come down to a modern abstract sculpture on a plinth. Go sharp right, and almost immediately left through the second gap in the handrail down the slope to the road. Cross to the sea-side of the road *[19. 06.57'/33.97', 4.19km/550m].* Down to the left, on the rocks above the sea, you will see a concrete platform. This is the base for Mitilini's group of year-round swimmers, and at any time of year,

in any weather, you are likely to see people swimming. (The official municipal bathing beach, with paid-for facilities, is two hundred metres back along the road to the right).

Go to the left along the road, which follows the cliff-edge on the right, and the outer walls of the castle high above on the left. You soon pass a white building on the headland to your right *[20. 06.69'/34.00', 4.45km/260m].* This is a lighthouse signalling the northern approach to Mitilini harbour: in recent years it has been renovated and modernised. (The group of homeless dogs that lives here is fed by local animal-lovers, who have also provided basic shelters dotted around the headland. As a result the dogs are friendly, relatively healthy, and give every appearance of enjoying their lives.)

Continue along the road. The castle defences come down to the cliff edge, and just before the road leads out through the lower entrance gate back into Epano Skala you will see on the left a small hamam, which at the time of writing was undergoing restoration *[21. 06.77'/33.59', 5.10km/650m].*

Go through the ruined castle gate on to the main road *[22. 06.76'/33.54', 5.19km/90m].* Keep right along past the harbour-side tavernas to return to your starting-point *[23. 06.72'/33.37', 5.46km/270m],* or pause here for a meal.

Mitilini: Places of Interest

Numbers refer to points on the walk.

Epano Skala (Επάνω Σκάλα)

Epano Skala, the ancient port of Mitilini, occupied the whole of the wide bay between what is now the northern gate of the castle, and the derelict factory on the opposite shore. The protecting breakwaters, dating from the 5th century AD, which can still be seen just above sea-level, total 500 metres in length, and were once supplemented by a third which formed an inner harbour. The harbour is now only used by a few small fishing boats, and a small boat repair yard tucked below the castle walls.

On land, directly opposite the harbour, was the commercial hub of the ancient city - the market area, or agora, of which the excavated **Loggia**, or **Stoa**, formed a part **(1)**.

A short distance away towards the castle, there is a reconstructed section of the massive harbour works, which were uncovered on this site in the late 1990s during the building of a new city drainage system.

The Ottoman Legacy

Under Ottoman rule, Epano Skala became a predominantly Ottoman and Muslim area of the city. Understandably, after the expulsion of the Ottoman rulers in 1912, preservation of their buildings became a low priority, and many were used as quarries for building materials. It is only in the last ten to fifteen years that their historic interest has overcome patriotic emotion and restoration and conservation work has begun.

The remains of three mosques survive here:

2. Yali Camii: This was built about 1880, on the site of an earlier mosque, dating from 1690, which was destroyed in an earthquake in 1867. Its minaret, which was in the fenced-off grassy area to its right, collapsed in 1939. It is the only mosque whose building survives more or less intact, and now houses a horticultural supplier.

3. Yeni Camii (New Mosque): Built in 1825, it was the largest and last new mosque to be built in the city. It was a square building in the Turkish-Byzantine style with dome (The roof was demolished after the Great War and the materials sold.) Its minaret, of which

only the base survives, was over 30 metres high. The shell of the building has been conserved to prevent further deterioration, and is now occasionally used for exhibitions and cultural events.

Valide Camii: This is the only mosque in Mitilini with a surviving minaret, 15 metres high. It dates from before 1791, so is the oldest of the three, though its foundation stone, dated 1615, comes from an older building. This mosque is not included in the walk, but is a short distance from the start/finish point in Kornarou Str (Οδός Κορνάρου). This is the street running behind the Stoa: go along it to the right, and at the end of the site continue for about 120 metres. The mosque is on the right.

4. Tarsi Hamam ('Market Hamam'): This impressive 19th century bath-house was the first Ottoman building to be restored, in the late 1990s, and is now used for occasional cultural events.

Churches

5. Cathedral of St Athanasios (Αγ Αθανάσιος): Built in the late 16th century in the form of a three-aisle cruciform basilica, with a fretwork iconostasis (screen) from 1738 which some regard as one of the most impressive works of post-Byzantine art. The 19th century gothic bell-tower is 33 metres tall (the Ottoman building permit restricted its height to less than the minaret of the New Mosque).

The cathedral houses the relics of the patron saint of Mitilini, Ag Theodoros, and is the seat of the Metropolitan (bishop) of Mitilini.

7. St. Therapon (Αγ θεράπων): This is the largest church in Mitilini, and its dome dominates views of the city from all directions. It was built between 1880 and 1915, designed by the Lesvos architect Argyris Adalis and decorated by local artists and craftsmen. It is built to a traditional Orthodox cruciform plan, but the exterior shows many western influences, including neo-classical, baroque and gothic.

The Statue of Liberty

12. The Statue of Liberty, so-called for its resemblance to its namesake in New York, but also because it symbolises the freeing of Lesvos from Ottoman rule (the figure of Liberty is facing victoriously towards the coast of Turkey) is Lesvos's memorial to the victims of the Great War, which for Greece lasted from 1912 until 1922 – from the outbreak of war with the Ottoman Empire until her defeat in the Anatolian campaign against the new Turkey. The statue was cast in bronze from designs by Lesvos artist Georgios Iakovidis and erected in 1930.

The Archaeological Museums

13. The Old Museum: The mansion housing the old museum was built in 1912, but is in the style of the many 19th century mansions in Mitilini, Molivos, and elsewhere on Lesvos. It has been the museum since 1965, though the building was shared by the Ministry of the Aegean from 1985 to 1992. It has a large, well-organised and described collection from excavations across the island.

14. The New Museum: The new museum, in a purpose-built building, was completed in 1995. It houses a permanent exhibition on "Lesvos from the Hellenistic to Roman Times", which aims to give the visitor a picture of the life-style in Lesvos from the 2nd century BC to the 3rd century AD. The exhibition presents villas with artistic mosaic floors, sculptures and items of daily use.

Both museums are administered by the 20th Ephorate (Department) of Prehistoric and Classical Antiquities, part of the Greek Ministry of Culture.

Mitilini Castle

16. From its earliest days, the fortress of Mitilini was the largest and one of the most powerful in the Eastern Mediterranean. It dates back to AD 483-565, during the reign of the Emperor Justinian in the Byzantine period, but is believed to stand over the ancient Acropolis. It was expanded and developed by later rulers, especially the Genoese Gatelouzo dynasty and the Ottomans.

The castle is open to visitors, with bi-lingual plans and explanatory sign-boards at points of interest both inside and outside the walls.

Theofilos & Teriade Museums

Teriade (real name Stratis Eleftheriades) was a native of Mitilini who went to Paris in 1915 at the age of eighteen to study law. Instead he became an art critic, patron, and, most importantly, publisher.

From 1937 to 1975 he commissioned most of the significant artists of the first half of the century

to produce series of works for his quarterly journal 'Verve' or the later 'Grands Livres'.

The results are displayed in Vareia in sixteen rooms over two floors of the mansion which he gave to the city in 1979.

"..lithographs, engravings, woodblock prints and watercolours by the likes of Miró, Chagall, Picasso,

Matisse, Le Corbusier, Léger, Roualt and Villon...an astonishing collection for a relatively remote Aegean island, and one which deserves a leisurely perusal."

(Marc Dubin, Rough Guide to the Dodecanese and the East Aegean)

A smaller building in the grounds houses the Theofilos Museum, devoted to the works of the famous local naive painter Theofilos Hatzimihaïl (1868-1934), who was discovered and supported in his later years by Teriade.

From Karini to the Roman Aqueduct of Paspala

6

Total distance 7½ kilometres

 Walking time 2½ hours

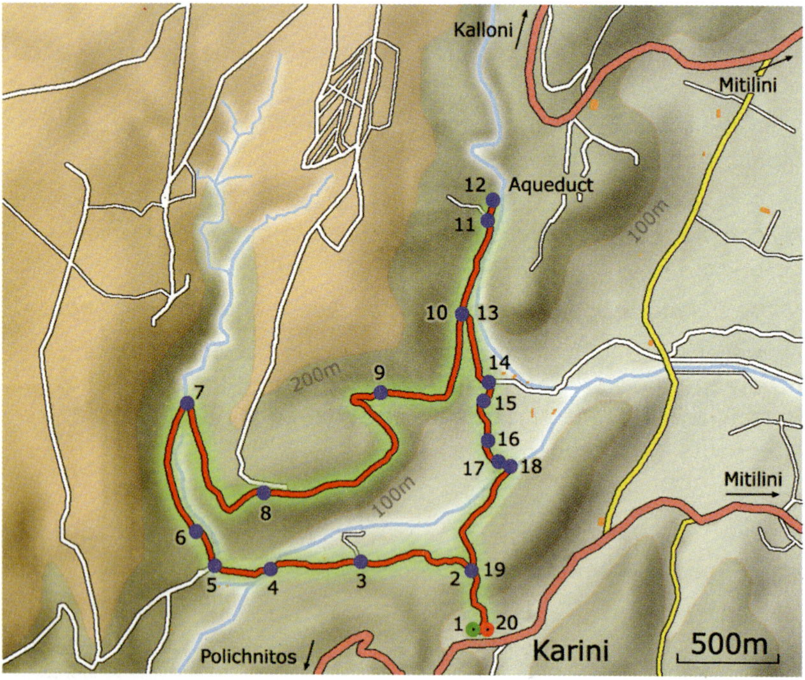

This walk takes you from Karini to the remains of the Roman aqueduct at Paspala, near Lambou Miloi. Part of the 26km aqueduct built around the end of the 1st century BC, it is less accessible and well known than the section at Moria, but in some ways a more dramatic sight, with four tall arches bridging a deep wooded ravine.

The route leads through olive groves and pine forest, over ancient stone bridges and along river valleys, with stunning views across to the Olympos mountain range to enjoy on the way.

The cool and shady 'oasis' of Karini is on the road from Mitilini to

Polichnitos, 4¼km from its junction with the main Mitilini – Kalloni road. It was a resting-place for pilgrims on their way to Agiasos, before starting the steep final climb to their destination. A simple kafenion was established here, whose proprietor, the grandfather of the present owner, in about 1912 allowed the wandering primitive painter Theofilos Hatzimihaïl (1868-1934) to set up home in the hollow trunk of the massive plane tree next to the building. In gratitude Theofilos painted a series of murals on the outside and inside walls of the kafenion, and on the walls of the adjacent spring. The paintings have faded into near invisibility, but the hollow tree, spring, and kafenion are still there, together with a larger, more modern taverna, and roadside stalls selling local produce and handicrafts.

Karini is the starting point for the next two walks.

The walk starts from the signed parking area behind the kafenion and taverna, on the right-hand side of the road as you come from the direction of Mitilini *[1. 39°07.16'/26°23.31']*. Walk uphill on the concrete track away from Karini, continuing until you reach a crossing near the brow of the hill *[2. 07.31'/23.29', 310m, 7 min]*.

Turn left and follow the track downhill through olive groves. Ignore a track leading down to the right *[3. 07.35'/22.19', 930m/620m, 8 min]*, but continue to the foot of the hill and take the right fork,

where a short stretch of concrete leads across a stream next to an ancient stone bridge *[4. 07.32'/22.59', 1.30km/370m, 7 min]*. (If you prefer, you can keep left for a few metres at this junction and walk over the bridge.)

Follow the narrow track up to a T-junction and turn right *[5. 07.33'/22.40', 1.58km/280m, 5 min]*. Go along the track through the pine forest, passing a farm in the river valley on your right. It bends round to the left and rises to meet a much wider track *[6. 07.41'/22.34', 1.77km/190m, 5 min]*.

Turn right and continue along the side of the valley. Near the head of the valley the track bends sharply round to the right across a strip of concrete (which carries the river at times of high water) and climbs along the other side *[7. 07.76'/22.31', 2.43km/660m, 10 min]*.

At the next fork keep to the right, heading downhill *[8. 07.52'/22.57', 3.20km/770m, 10 min]*, and continue, with views across the valley on your right over unbroken forest to the peak of Mt Olympos and its surrounding mountain range. Ignore a track leading off downhill to the right *[9. 07.79'/22.97', 4.27km/1.07km, 17 min]*, but continue on the main track until it leads downhill, now with woodland on both sides, to reach a junction where another track goes off down to the right *[10. 07.97'/23.25', 4.93km/660m, 7 min]*.

Ignore this track for the present (you will be using it on your return from the aqueduct). Continue straight ahead on the main track as it begins to climb again. It bends left – looking ahead along the valley at this point you may catch your first glimpse of the arches of the aqueduct. Ahead, slightly to the right as you climb the hill, you will see the scar where the track turns sharp right across the end of a side valley. Now look for a small path coming in from the left. Opposite it, down the bank on your right, you will see a small ancient stone bridge. *[11. 08.22'/23.34', 5.38km/450m, 7 min].*

Go down to the bridge (there are traces of a path but it is more of a scramble!) and cross it with care – the bridge is sound but the surface is very uneven, with a drop of several metres on to the stony stream-bed below. (If you prefer not to tackle this section, stay on the track: it passes high above the end of the aqueduct, but the views are not nearly as good). At the end of the bridge keep to the right – there is a small but clear path running along the side of the valley which ends at the top of the aqueduct *[12. 08.26'/23.38', 5.43km/50m, 5 min].*

(Tempting though it may seem to the more intrepid of you, please do <u>not</u> attempt to walk along the top of the aqueduct. Though it may look like a smooth path, the third arch is missing, and there is a sheer drop into the river far below. And you are a long way from emergency services and mobile phone signals!)

Retrace your steps to the track, turn left and return to the junction at point 10 *[13. 07.97'/23.25', 5.92km/490m, 12 min].* Turn left, and follow this lesser track downhill. It turns left, and passes a chapel on the left. There is a farm on your left just ahead, but before you reach it turn right on to a footpath *[14. 07.81'/23.34', 6.30km/380m, 6 min].*

Follow the footpath. It soon opens out into an olive grove: go uphill diagonally to the right towards a farm building in a small enclosure *[15. 07.76'/23.33', 6.38km/80m, 4 min].* Keep the enclosure to your left, and go round it to pick up the path leading downhill towards a wall.

It leads to the left-hand end of the wall, and winds on, downhill at first, between fenced small-holdings to cross a small stream *[16. 07.67'/23.33', 6.51km/130m, 5 min].* The path continues along the far bank of the stream for a few metres, before turning right (ignore the small path off to the left through a gate immediately after this corner) and leading on through an olive grove to arrive at a river-bank *[17. 07.59'/23.38', 6.67km/160m, 5 min]*.

It is possible to cross the river at this point, at the risk of wet feet (you are heading for the track on the opposite bank), but we recommend turning left along the track for thirty metres until you spot an inconspicuous concrete bridge down on your right *[18. 07.60'/23.41', 6.70km/30m, 2 min]*.

Cross the bridge and turn right along the track on the other side. Follow it alongside the river, and then as it veers left uphill. Ignore a track off to the right, and continue uphill on the main track, which becomes concrete and steeper until it reaches a crossing *[19. 07.31'/23.29', 7.28km/580m, 15 min]*.

This was point 2 of the outward route. Go straight ahead over the brow of the hill and continue downhill to the end of your walk at the Karini parking area *[20. 07.16'/23.31', 7.59km/310m, 7 min]*.

From Karini to Asomatos and Agiasos

7

Total distance 9¼ kilometres

 Walking time 3½ hours

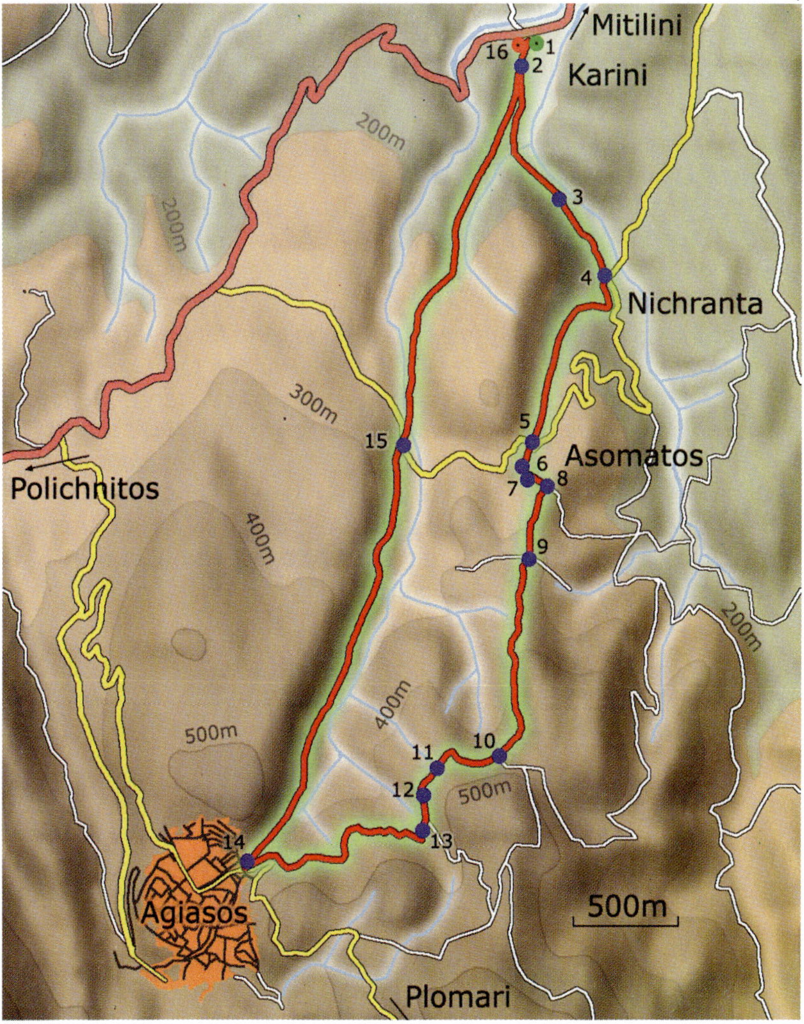

We have done our best in this book to give you a selection of walks showing you the many facets and beauties of Lesvos, and this walk has almost everything except the sea! Like Walk 6, it starts from Karini, it takes you along an idyllic river-side footpath, and then climbs through olive-groves to the traditional hill-village of Asomatos. Then it winds higher into the foothills of Mount Olympos on the way to the picturesque pilgrimage town of Agiasos, and finally returns on the 'pilgrims' path' a broad kalderimi leading almost straight downhill back to Karini. Along the way there are tranquil woodland glades and stunning mountain views, as well as opportunities to explore the hill towns of Asomatos and Agiasos itself.

Built 500 metres above sea level on the eastern slopes of Mount Olympos, Agiasos sits in a natural amphitheatre. Tradition says that the first settler here was Agathon from Ephesus who arrived in 802AD bearing an icon of the Virgin Mary painted by St Luke, and other holy relics, and built a hermitage nearby. In the 12th century this was replaced by a monastery housing the relics, and this became a place of pilgrimage, attracting the faithful from as far away as the Greek communities of Asia Minor. The town grew up around the monastery largely to serve the pilgrims, hence the local craft traditions of pottery and wood-carving which survive to this day. (It is said that the first kiln was constructed in the hermitage of Agathon, who himself had a working knowledge of the ceramic arts prior to his arrival to Agiasos, and that the area's first ceramic wares were produced there in the 8th -9th centuries.) With the decline of agriculture and pilgrimage during the second half of the

20th century the town's population declined from its peak of over 7,000 to around 2,500 today, and although the festival of the Virgin on 15 August is still an important event in the local calendar, the town is now dependent more on day visits by overseas holiday-makers. While depopulation and the resulting empty and collapsing buildings have given the town a somewhat melancholy air, it is still a beautiful and fascinating place for a visit, especially the walled monastic church of the Virgin (Παναγία), with its surrounding complex of monastic cells and small Byzantine and Folk museums.

The walk starts on the road about 100 metres downhill from the entrance to the Karini 'oasis', where a broad kalderimi runs uphill alongside an abandoned olive press (on the left coming from the direction of Mitilini) *[1. 39°07.15'/26°23.39'].*

Walk up the kalderimi: very soon you will see a path forking off to the left [2. 07.08'/23.36', 110m, 3 min]. Take this path, and follow it through olive groves. It bends left and leads up and over a rocky mound before descending to a stream (The path is not immediately obvious at the beginning of this stretch: keep the stone wall on your left, and do not be led astray into the olive grove on the other side of the wall).

Turn right along the stream and follow the path along its bank until it veers up to the right (you may notice a faint path continuing ahead at this point) [3. 06.75'/23.48', 695m/585m, 15 min].

Take the clear path uphill. When you come to a small farm building on the right, with a gated olive grove immediately ahead, bear left and continue alongside the olive grove. The path descends and emerges on a road: there is a water fountain on your right, and downhill to your left a group of large buildings around a yard, formerly an olive mill [4. 06.56'/23.62', 955m/260m, 10 min].

Turn right on to the road, and then immediately fork right again on to a kalderimi. It winds up through olive groves, passing an old chapel sheltering under a large oak tree on the left. You eventually reach a water fountain on the right, dated 1883, but now built into a high stone wall below a large modern building up above. This is the primary school of Asomatos, which also houses a Centre of Environmental Education, founded in 2002 with the aim of raising environmental awareness among students, both throughout Lesvos and nationally.

The kalderimi bends right and left and immediately reaches a crossing with a concrete street [5. 06.14'/23.39', 1.82km/865m, 20 min]. Go straight across and up the steep cobbled street leading into the centre of Asomatos. At the next crossing go straight again, with the village church in its large courtyard on your right, and then take the first turning to the left [6. 06.08'/23.35', 1.92km/100m, 5 min].

Follow the street up to a T-junction and turn left [7. 06.06'/23.36', 1.97km/50m, 3 min]. Then continue up to a crossing at the brow of the hill, where there is a brown-painted chapel on the right, and the village cemetery on the left at the other side of the crossing [8. 06.04'/23.45', 2.09km/120m, 3 min].

(If you have already done the Agii Anargyri to Asomatos and

Taxiarches walk, and this point seems familiar, it is point 5 on that route. Almost the next 2km is common to both routes, but to avoid confusion we will repeat the instructions here.)

Turn right up the concrete street in front of the chapel, and almost immediately left again up a narrow concrete footpath. The concrete ends, and the path continues to wind up to the brow of the hill (be careful not to trip over the raised water-pipe inspection cover here!). At the next junction go straight ahead *[9. 05.86'/23.38', 2.44km/350m, 10 min]*, and when the path forks keep right up a narrow, rough, stony stretch, steep in places, with stunning views across to the left.

Then bear right on to a rare level section along olive-grove terracing, with the white peak of Mt Olympos ahead to the right. The path leads uphill again along the edge of a deep valley. It climbs steadily, with the occasional brief downhill section, following the end of the valley round to the right, until it reaches a T-junction *[10. 05.37'/23.29', 3.36km/920m, 30 min]*.

Turn right. The path leads up again; behind you across the valley are high sheer cliffs bare even of the pine trees growing on the lower slopes. Cross the ridge ahead and bear round to the left to join a track *[11. 05.34'/23.08', 3.68km/320m, 10 min]*.

Keep left along the track. Now Olympos is to the right of you across the valley again, with the town of Agiasos on its lower slopes. Look for a small path leading down to the right *[12. 05.27'/23.04', 3.83km/150m, 3 min]*.

Go down the path, taking great care: it is very steep and stony. At the bottom it joins a track: go left and immediately right *[13. 05.19'/23.03', 3.98km/150m, 7 min]*. When the track comes to an end continue ahead on the path, uphill on rock, through oaks, chestnuts, beeches and strawberry trees. Agiasos comes into view ahead as the path continues downhill over rock, then kalderimi. It bends round to the right then climbs again, and finally levels out on concrete as it reaches the edge of the town. It passes classic old houses up on the left, and the ruins of a large olive press below on the right. In a garden on the right you may see a collection of old olive-oil jars, some of them hand-decorated.

The path finally emerges on to a paved street *[14. 05.11'/22.46', 5.04km/1.06km, 30 min]*. Go uphill to the left to explore Agiasos, and then return here to continue your walk. (Distances and timings continue from here.)

Turn right down the broad paved street. This is the 'patomeni' (πατωμένη), the kalderimi that brings pilgrims uphill all the way from Karini on the final stage of their journey to worship at the church of the Virgin Mary (Παναγία) on August 15th each year. It runs down along the edge of a deep valley, the precipitous slopes opposite thickly planted with olive trees interspersed with outcrops of volcanic rock.

When you arrive at a road go across (the kalderimi runs across the road) *[15. 06.14′/22.96′, 7.18km/2.14km, 30 min],* and continue steeply down the other side. Go on through olive groves as the track levels out and crosses a bridge over a stream. The kalderimi becomes patchy for a short distance, but then returns in good condition for the final downhill stretch back to your starting point at Karini *[16. 07.15′/23.39′, 9.22km/2.04km, 30 min].*

An Ascent of Olympos from Agiasos

Total distance 10½ kilometres

 Walking time 4 hours

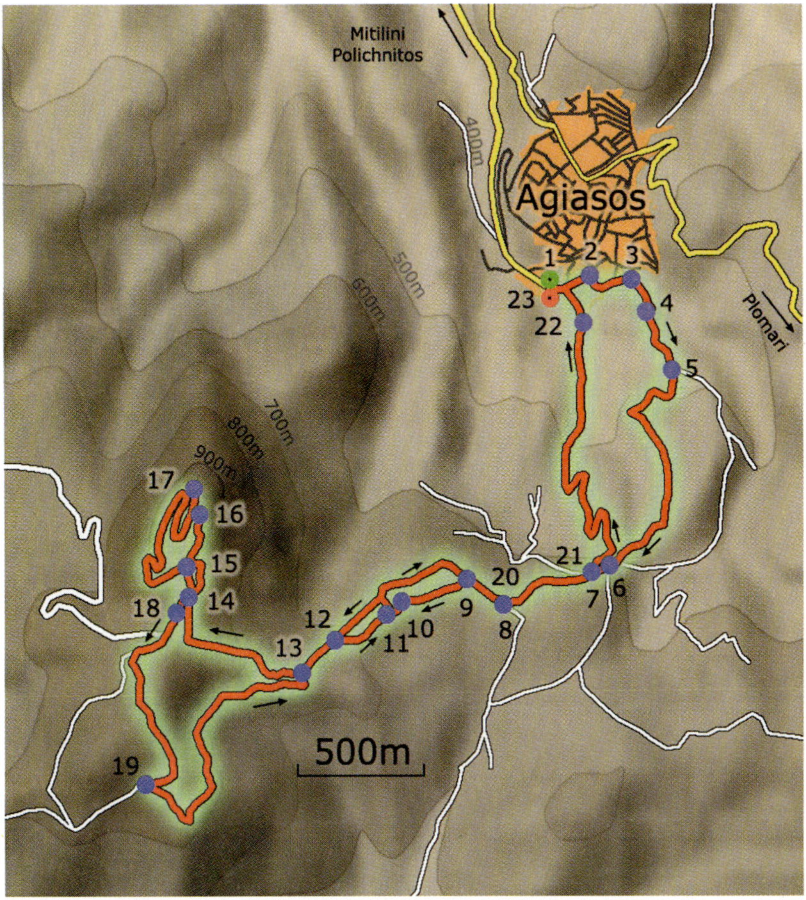

Mitilini
Polichnitos

Agiasos

Piomari

500m

This walk takes you from Agiasos to the summit of Mount Olympos, at 968 metres the joint highest peak on Lesvos (it shares the title with Vigla in the Lepetimnos range in the north of the island). It is not nearly such a daunting undertaking as it may sound: your 'base camp' in Agiasos is at about 400m, making the total climb around 570 metres, most of it on untaxing gradients along kalderimi and small footpaths through the shade of beech and oak woodland. On the way you will enjoy stunning views of the great white mountain, and while, when you arrive, the summit itself cannot be called beautiful – it is dominated by the buildings and masts of a television transmitter – the views across the island and beyond in every direction are spectacular and not to be missed.

At the time of writing the upward route of this walk was well signposted. However several of the signs have collapsed or are almost illegible, and there are also other signposted routes in the area. To avoid confusion we have ignored the signs in our description: please do likewise and don't be tempted to rely on them.

Olympos is also known as Profitis Ilias (Προφήτης Ηλίας), the name given in Greece to the highest point in any area. In English, Profitis Ilias is the Old Testament Prophet Elijah, who was taken up to heaven in a whirlwind from a mountain-top, hence his association with high places. However it is thought that when Christianity was brought to Greece some of the ancient Greek gods were co-opted into the new religion to make it more palatable to potential converts. Among others, Apollo, god of the Sun (Ilios – Ήλιος in Greek), was identified with Elijah, so Profitis Ilias could also be seen as the prophet of the sun.

Agiasos is a beautiful and fascinating town (see the description in Walk 7) which is well worth exploring. We recommend that you make this a full-day excursion, lunching at one of the local tavernas

after completing your walk, and rounding off the day with a wander round the town and some shopping at the many local wood-craft and ceramic workshops.

Agiasos lies 3km south of the main road from Mitilini to Polichnitos. The junction is 8km from the turning to Polichnitos on the Mitilini – Kalloni main road, and from the other direction 21½km from Polichnitos.

Your starting point is the bus shelter in the parking area [*1. 39°04.81'/26°22.21'*]. Walk uphill towards the town, past tavernas across the road on your left, and the local museum to your right. As the road narrows and begins to climb to the left towards the town centre, turn right down ΟΔΟΣ ΚΗΠΩ ΠΑΝΑΓΙΑΣ (Garden of the Virgin Mary) [*2. 04.84'/22.32', 160m, 3 min*].

The street leads down to the church of ΖΩΟΔΟΧΟΣ ΠΗΓΗ (The Lifegiving Spring) on the left, and then bears left. Follow it round, ignoring a street up to the right, and then, at the next junction, in front of a row of garages, go to the right. [*3. 04.84'/22.42', 335m/175m, 5 min*].

Almost immediately, go right on to a paved path (not the concrete one next to it). Go straight ahead at the next crossing, and when you come to a T-junction go to the left up a kalderimi *[4. 04.77'/22.46', 515m/180m, 5 min]*. It winds uphill, passing a concrete barn on the left, and shortly afterwards divides *[5. 04.66'/22.54', 780m/265m, 7 min]*.

Keep right and continue up on kalderimi. It ends temporarily on a comparatively level stretch of path, where there are clear views of the upper reaches of Olympos over to the right, then resumes, leading back uphill through beech woods to end near a spring and water-trough set in a wall under a large plane tree *[6. 04.26'/22.36', 1.80km/1.02km, 30 min]*.

From the spring, go to the right, and turn left on to a track, which immediately joins a wider track coming from the left. Go straight ahead, and then almost immediately fork left up the first of two paths *[7. 04.26'/22.32', 1.90km/100m, 3 min]*. Follow the path until it meets a track, and turn right *[8. 04.18'/22.08', 2.32km/420m, 12 min]*. (Try to remember this junction – you will be using it on the return journey.)

Walk along the track until the first junction on the left, where a lesser track goes off at right angles *[9. 04.23'/21.98',*

2.49km/170m, 2 min]. Turn left and go down the steep hill (there is a kalderimi on the left). At the bottom of the hill bear right on to a kalderimi path, leaving the track, which swings to the left through metal gates. Go up the path, with an unusually smart farm below to the right, until it comes out on to another narrow track. (The path may be blocked by fallen trees near the top, but it is easy to find a way round them.) *[10. 04.19'/21.81', 2.70km/210m, 8 min].*

Cross the track (it leads to a farm a few metres to your left) and continue on the path, which ends with a steep climb up to meet a wide track *[11. 04.16'/21.78', 2.77km/70m, 4 min].* Go diagonally to the left across the track, continue up the path opposite, and where this meets another path leading downhill to the right (you may see a yellow trekking trail sign on a tree a short distance down) keep on to the left. The path starts to descend: it leads through a gate and down to a dirt road *[12. 04.11'/21.64', 2.99km/220m, 10 min].*

Turn right on to the road and follow it uphill for about 180 metres. Look for a path leading up the bank on the right *[13. 04.05'/21.54', 3.17km/180m, 4 min].*

Go up the path, and when it comes to a junction with several other paths take the widest, which leads uphill to the right. Follow this rocky path uphill through lichen-covered holly-oak. You will get occasional views of the bare flank of Olympos looming ahead of you to the right. The path eventually joins an asphalt road opposite a large barn *[14. 04.19'/21.22', 3.83km/660m, 20 min].*

Turn right on to the road, and after a few metres look for a small path going up to the left through the trees. When it rejoins the road (at the time of writing this stretch had not yet been asphalted) cross and go up the bank opposite on to a kalderimi path *[15. 04.26'/21.22', 3.96km/130m, 5 min].*

The kalderimi winds up the face of the mountain towards the summit (if you would prefer not to tackle this stretch the road also leads there, and is your return route. In any case we do not recommend this path in wet or misty conditions). Several sections have been covered by falling rock chippings from above, but in general the path is still clear and not difficult to negotiate. It ends at a concrete track immediately below the summit *[16. 04.37'/21.25', 4.19km/180m, 12 min].*

Turn left, and immediately right. Go past the transmitting station to reach the chapel of Profitis Ilias, the tall memorial cross, and the fire observation post *[17. 04.40'/21.24', 4.31km/120m, 4 min]*. (If the gate to the observation post is open, take extra care if you venture through. The platform is unfenced, and it's a long hard way down!)

To return from the peak, walk back down the road (this is the dirt road protected by crash barriers, not the concrete track you came up) as far as the barn, and continue for a few metres until a track forks off to the left *[18. 04.18'/21.20', 5.57km/1.26km, 17 min]*.

Take the track. At the first junction, where a track goes downhill to the right, keep left, at the next fork left over a ridge, and at the third go left again *[19. 03.82'/21.10', 6.50km/930m, 13 min]*.

Stay on this track. You may recognise a short stretch from your outward route (from point 13 to point 12). You will later come to the steep track, now on the right, which you went down on the way out (point 9), and finally the junction with the path that you came up from the spring (point 8). (If you see a finger-post pointing left to Agiasos before you get here, ignore it) *[20. 04.18'/22.08', 8.58km/2.08km, 40 min]*.

Turn left down the path, and when you reach the track at the bottom follow it to the right *[21. 04.26'/22.32', 9.00km/420m, 10 min]*. Almost immediately keep left on the downhill track past the spring, which will now be on your right. Stay on the track as it winds down into a forested valley. It is very steep in places: the steepest parts are on concrete. It eventually becomes a wide kalderimi and you pass a terraced property planted with fruit trees on your right.

You begin to get glimpses of Agiasos ahead of you. At a crossing continue ahead, then at the next fork go left downhill into a concrete lane (there is a large derelict industrial building on the junction) *[22. 04.75'/22.30', 10.20km/1.20km, 25 min]*.

The lane emerges into the parking area at the foot of the town. Turn left for a few metres to return to the bus shelter where your walk began *[23. 04.81'/22.21', 10.40km/200m, 5 min]*, or right to go into the town.

From Agii Anargyri to Asomatos and Taxiarches

Total distance 5¾ kilometres

 Walking time 3¼ hours

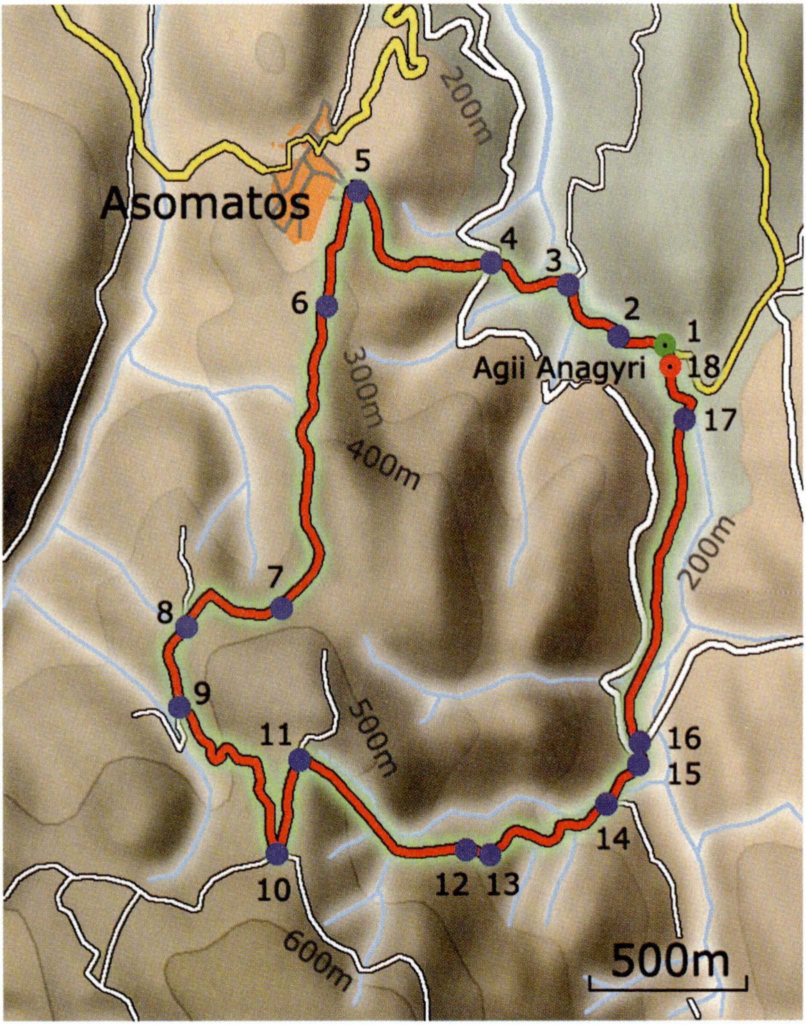

Asomatos

Agii Anagyri

500m

This walk takes you through the north-eastern foothills of the Olympus mountain range, much of the way on well-maintained cobbled kalderimi. It leads through olive groves, and past chapels to the hill village of Asomatos.

One of the most beautiful, but least visited villages on Lesvos, Asomatos is believed to date from the 13th century, and is now officially protected as a 'traditional village', with its original winding cobbled streets, stone houses, and water fountains.

From Asomatos you continue to climb into chestnut woods, with beautiful mountain views on the way, before descending again to return past the chapel of Taxiarches (Ταξιάρχες – Archangels).

Your starting point is Agii Anargyri. Agii Anargyri (Άγιοι Ανάργυροι) means 'holy unmercenaries', saints who received no payment for their medical services, and is the collective name of saints Kosmas and Damianos. There is a beautiful chapel here, built in 1881 over springs in a shady glade near a stream. There are picnic tables, ample parking space, and a taverna which is sometimes open during the summer.

*This is a comparatively short, but strenuous walk, involving a
number of steep ascents and descents (which experienced walkers
will know can be more tiring than the climbs!). Agii Anargyri is
150m above sea level, and at its highest the route reaches 540m
(near point 11), giving a difference in altitude of almost 400m.*

*The easiest way to reach Agii Anargyri is to take the turning to
Polichnitos and Vatera about 13km from Mitilini on the main road to
Kalloni, and where it bends sharp right after almost three kilometres
go straight ahead on the road signposted to Asomatos. After about
one kilometre turn left on the side road signposted to Agii Anargyri
and follow the signs for another 2¾km.*

Start from the parking area in front of the church of Agii Anargyri
[1. 39°05.77'/26°24.13']. Walk down, with the buildings and springs
on your right, and take the footpath at the end of the open area.
After a few metres the path forks: keep left downhill and then right
alongside a stream to reach a footbridge *[2. 05.81'/24.01', 195m,
7 min]*.

Go across the bridge and turn right at the end. When you come

to the beginning of a kalderimi leading uphill to the left, take this, ignoring a small path down to the right *[3. 05.89′/23.90′, 395m/200m, 6 min].*

The kalderimi crosses the head of a valley and winds uphill to join a track by a chapel (dedicated to Παναγιά Γλυκοφιλώσα, Panagia Glykofilosa – Our Lady of the Sweet Kiss) *[4. 05.92′/23.75′, 615m/220m, 10 min].* Cross the track diagonally to the left, and rejoin the kalderimi as it continues up to the right.

Continue climbing, passing another chapel on the left, followed by a stone water fountain, where the climb and kalderimi both end very briefly. Then go on uphill, on kalderimi once more, until you reach a crossing at the brow of the hill. There is a brown-painted chapel on the corner ahead, and, less obviously, a cemetery above you on the right *[5. 06.04′/23.45′, 1.05km/400m, 20 min].*

(If you have already done the Agii Anargyri to Asomatos and Taxiarches walk, and this point seems familiar, it is point 8 on that route. Almost the next 2km is common to both routes, but to avoid confusion we will repeat the instructions here.)

This is the beginning of the small hill town of Asomatos, which is down the cobbled street ahead of you. To continue the walk, however, turn left up the concrete street, and almost immediately left again up a narrow concrete footpath. The concrete ends, and a narrow path continues to wind up to the brow (be careful not to trip over the raised water-pipe inspection cover here!). At the next junction go straight ahead *[6. 05.86'/23.38', 1.40km/350m, 10 min]*, and when the path forks keep right up a narrow, rough, stony stretch, steep in places, with stunning views across to the left.

Then bear right on to a rare level section along olive-grove terracing, with the white peak of Mt Olympos ahead to the right. The path leads uphill again along the edge of a deep valley. It climbs steadily, with the occasional brief downhill section, following the end of the valley round to the right, until it reaches a T-junction *[7. 05.37'/23.29', 2.32km/920m, 30 min]*.

Turn right. The path leads up again; behind you across the valley are high sheer cliffs bare even of the pine trees growing on the lower slopes. Cross the ridge ahead and bear round to the left to join a track *[8. 05.34'/23.08', 2.64km/320m, 10 min]*.

Keep left along the track. Now Olympos is to the right of you across the valley again, with the town of Agiasos on its lower slopes. Ignore a path off to the right, and when the track divides keep left uphill *[9. 05.21'/23.06', 2.88km/240m, 5 min]*.

It winds steeply uphill (the steepest parts are concrete in places) through chestnut trees to a crossing *[10. 04.97'/23.27', 3.56km/680m, 10 min]*. Turn left on to a wide kalderimi, ignoring the one leading ahead, and continue to the next junction, where a track joins diagonally from the right, and a path leads off downhill, also to the right *[11. 05.12'/23.32', 3.83km/270m, 5 min]*.

Take the path. It is a steep kalderimi winding downhill. The stones are often covered in a deep layer of fallen leaves, and can be deceptive and very slippery, especially when wet: take extra care. The kalderimi ends briefly on a level stretch past a spring on the right, and emerges on a track *[12. 04.98'/23.68', 4.20km/370m, 20 min]*.

Follow the track to the right for a short distance, then go back to the left on to the kalderimi as it continues downhill *[13. 04.97'/23.73', 4.26km/60m, 2 min]*, and carry on down until you arrive at another track *[14. 05.04'/23.99', 4.51km/250m, 30 min]*.

Turn left on to the track and walk along until you see a chapel in the trees just below you on the right *[15. 05.11'/24.05', 4.65km/140m, 3 min]*. This is Taxiarches (Ταξιάρχες – Archangels).

Go down past the front of the chapel and follow the path round to the left and on downhill. At the next junction continue ahead, ignoring the path down to the right *[16. 05.14'/24.06', 4.69km/40m, 3 min]*.

The path leads through woodland, and then along the side of a valley into an olive grove, with the trees growing in individual semi-circular walled terraces. It descends towards the bottom of the valley to a bridge *[17. 05.68'/24.15', 5.61km/920m, 25 min]*. Go right across the bridge, turn left, left again when you meet a concrete road, and walk down to Agii Anargyri and the end of your walk *[18. 05.77'/24.13', 5.72km/110m, 5 min]*.

Achladeri, the Pesas waterfalls, and the Gulf of Kalloni

10

Total distance 10½ kilometres

Walking time 3 hours

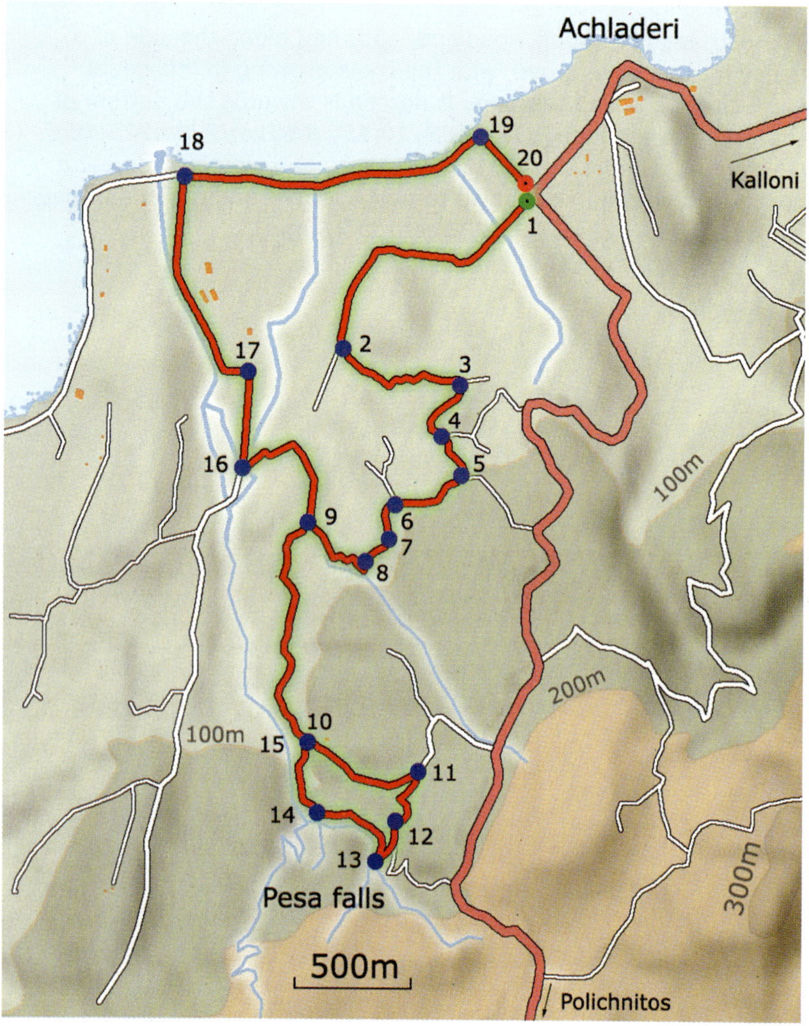

This is an easy 3 hour walk through olive groves and pine forest to the beautiful Pesas waterfalls, returning through farm-land and along the shore of the Gulf of Kalloni. The falls normally flow throughout the year, although increasing water extraction for irrigation from the springs above them means that you will sometimes find them dry. Starting near Achladeri, where the beach taverna is an ideal place for an after-walk drink or meal, it climbs gently from sea-level to approximately 120 metres, with almost continuous views over the gulf.

The walk starts and finishes on the main Kalloni – Polichnitos road approximately 1 km south of Achladeri, where it makes a right-angle turn. A wide dirt road leads towards the sea from this point: park on this road and return to the junction, where a wide track leads to the right through a pair of steel gates. **(These gates are usually kept closed and locked during the olive harvesting season from November to early January, when this walk is not possible.)**

Take the track from the junction *[1. 39°09.00'/26°16.32']* through the gates, and follow it, at first through level olive groves on both sides. It crosses a stream, and craggy rising ground begins to appear on the left. Where the track divides, with the route ahead

going through gates across a stream, turn left on to the minor track *[2. 08.61'/15.75', 1.24km, 17 min]*.

Follow it gently uphill through the olive grove, at first alongside a fence on the right, and then meandering on upward more steeply until it divides at the approach to the brow of the hill *[3. 08.59'/16.10', 1.83km/590m, 16 min]*. Ignore the path leading ahead, and bear right on the clearer track and continue to climb. It bears left, leading towards an open, grassy area at the brow of the hill. Bear right here on to a path leading diagonally uphill towards a belt of pine trees *[4. 08.46'/16.04', 2.16km/330m, 6 min]*.

Follow the path through the trees, out into another grassy area, and turn right on to a wider path *[5. 08.38'/16.11', 2.34km/180m, 6 min]*. Follow this path and continue on it as it bends left and right

downhill until you come to a gap between a holly-oak on the left and a low stone wall on the right [6. 08.31'/15.91', 2.67km/330m, 5 min]. Go through the gap, and continue on the path. Wind downhill with views of the Gulf of Kalloni, and then, when the path divides, drop down to the right over a terrace, with dense bushes below [7. 08.24'/15.90', 2.84km/170m, 7 min]. Keep left along under the terrace towards a rocky wall, and then follow round to the right to a small open area. (This spot, together with others along the route, is a favourite place for hunters, and is usually littered with spent shot-gun cartridges). Follow the path ahead over a collapsed wall, and then right to a ruined stone shed [8. 08.19'/15.83', 2.98km/140m, 5 min].

Take the path leading down to the left in front of the shed; follow it down to a stream and then right along the bank. The path goes left to cross the stream and leads on to the right and then left up to a T-junction with a track [9. 08.27'/15.66', 3.36km/380m, 5 min].

Turn left along the track until the next junction [10. 07.80'/15.67', 4.36km/1.00km, 16 min]. Keep left (signposted ΠΗΓΕΣ ΠΕΣΣΑ) and walk up through pine forest, passing a large concrete water cistern on the left, to reach another junction Turn right here (there is a hand-carved sign to 'Πηγές Πεσάς Μικροι καταρρακτες. Pessa springs small waterfalls'). [11. 07.75'/15.98', 4.76km/400m, 10 min].

Follow the track until it bends left uphill, then take the path leading down to the right with a wooden handrail and steps [12. 07.64'/15.92', 5.05km/290m, 5 min]. (Take care along these paths, especially where wooden log footbridges lead over small streams. On our last visit the condition of the steps and bridges was deteriorating, with some logs rotten or missing.) Where the path divides go down to the right, (going left will take you above the falls) and continue, ignoring the next steep path down right, to a viewing point and seat alongside the falls, which make an excellent excuse for a rest and a drink [13. 07.55'/15.86', 5.23km/180m, 5 min].

From the viewpoint retrace your steps to the steep downhill path (now on the left!). Follow it down into the valley and along the bank of the stream. (There is a picnic area here if you feel like a longer break). When the path meets a track at a T-junction turn right [14. 07.66'/15.69', 5.66km/430m, 8 min] and walk uphill to the next junction *[15. 07.80'/15.67', 5.95km/290m, 4 min]*.

This is the same junction as point 10. Turn left, (signposted ΚΑΜΠΟΣ), and retrace your steps as far as point 9. Then continue on the track; it leads downhill towards the gulf, and at the bottom of the hill swings left (ignore the track to the right leading into an olive grove). Continue to the next T-junction and turn right *[16. 08.39'/15.46', 7.58km/1.63km, 23 min]*.

You are now in the flat, fertile farm-land bordering the Gulf of Kalloni. Turn left at the next junction (the track straight ahead is a dead-end leading to a farm) *[17. 08.61'/15.48', 7.98km/400m, 6 min]*, and then follow the track round to the right as it runs alongside a river.

The track passes through a farm, with buildings on both sides, and continues straight ahead until it reaches the dirt road running along the shore of the gulf *[18. 09.04'/15.29', 8.93km/950m, 11 min]*. Turn right (signposted ΑΧΛΑΔΕΡΗ), and walk along between reed-beds and the sea until the road turns sharp right inland *[19. 09.13'/16.16', 10.20km/1.27km, 21 min]*.

Follow it, and walk inland for a final four minutes to return to your starting point *[20. 09.00'/16.32', 10.50km/300m, 4 min]*.

From the Hot Springs of Lisvori via the old watermill to Skamnioudi

Total distance 12¾ kilometres

 Walking time 3½ hours

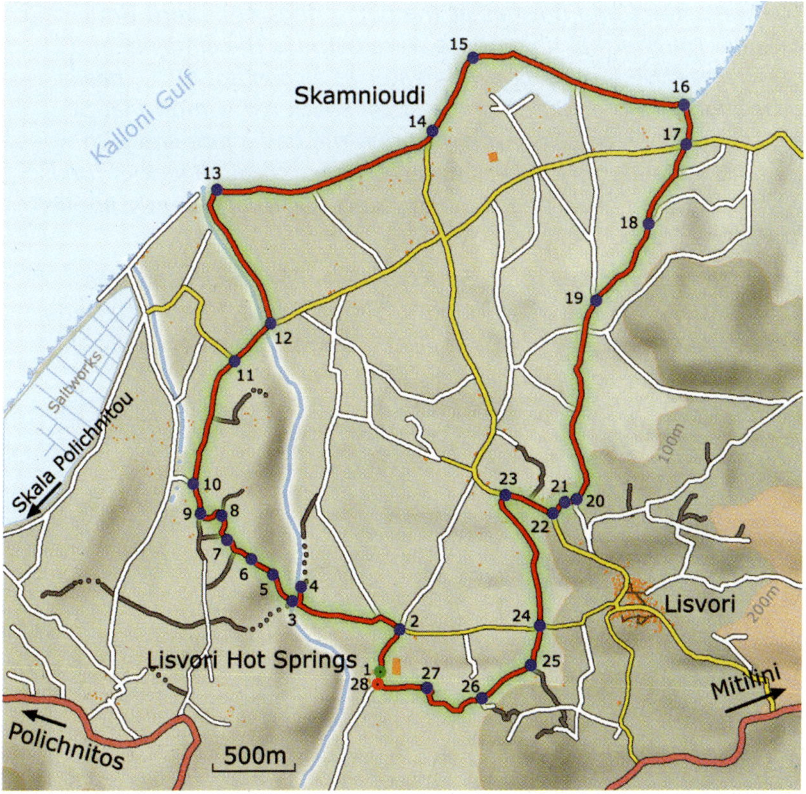

Skamnioudi

Kalloni Gulf

Skala Polichnitou

Saltworks

Lisvori Hot Springs

Lisvori

Mitilini

Polichnitos

500m

This is a walk rich in the agricultural and natural history of southern Lesvos, in the course of which you will enjoy stunning views over the Gulf of Kalloni, see the remains of an old water-mill and threshing floor, visit the unspoilt fishing harbour of Skamnioudi (where you can pause for a meal or refreshments at one of the harbour-side tavernas), and then pass through the site of the ancient city of Pyrrha, one of the founding city-states of Lesvos, and, according to archaeological discoveries the largest in area. You will walk along a beach, ideal for a mid-walk swim, which is backed by a seasonal lake rich in wading birds and wildfowl, and finally return on a kalderimi through olive groves which reputedly contain the oldest trees in Lesvos. Lisvori is also noted for the cultivation of broad beans and cumin, and also of anis, the main flavouring ingredient of ouzo.

The walk starts and finishes at the hot springs of Lisvori. Until recently the thermal baths here were perhaps the simplest and most attractive on Lesvos, with water at a constant 69°C, basic overnight accommodation and a small snack bar. Unfortunately extensive modernisation work to bring the baths into line with European standards appears to have stalled through lack of funds, and at the time of writing they are closed, with apparently no imminent prospect of re-opening.

To reach them, follow the road from Mitilini or Kalloni towards Polichnitos, and take the turning to Lisvori about 1½km after you pass through the village of Vassilika (4½km before Polichnitos).

Go through Lisvori, turning right and then left where you see signs to the Thermal Baths (take care, the streets are narrow, with very sharp turns). The baths are about 1½km further on.

Start at the entrance to the thermal baths *[1. 39°06.08'/26°12.08']*. Walk up the road, away from the bridge, as far as the first junction, where the asphalt road swings to the right *[2. 06.22'/12.17', 330m, 4 min]*.

Turn left, and follow a track through olive groves. At the next junction ignore the track off to the right, and subsequent lesser side tracks, but continue straight ahead until the track reaches a wire-mesh gate before crossing a stream *[3. 06.29'/11.74', 983m/653m, 8 min]*. Before crossing the stream turn right on a path along the bank for 100 metres to reach the ruins of Lisvori's old water-mill *[4. 06.34'/11.77', 1.09km/107m, 2 min]*.

Return to the gate, go through it and across the stream. Turn right on to a path leading uphill, and follow it until it ends at a field gate *[5. 06.37'/11.66', 1.40km/310m, 9 min]*. Go left into the field, and uphill through a gap in a wall towards the belt of trees at the

top. Behind you on the hillside across the valley lies the village of Lisvori. Head for the farm buildings at the top right-hand corner of the field, and when you reach them (by a well with an old, rusty, but working hand-pump), go down to the right and through a pair of gates, then left on to a footpath leading downhill *[6. 06.41'/11.57', 1.56km/160m, 4 min].* The path bends left and continues downhill. Look out for old stone-cut water-troughs and a circular stone-paved threshing floor in a field to your left *[7. 06.48'/11.48', 1.64km/80m, 8 min].*

When the path divides at a ruined farmhouse, go on downhill to the right – you may encounter several substantial brushwood barriers along this section – find a way round them if possible, or move and replace them carefully. The path comes to a T-junction; turn left and continue downhill *[8. 06.57'/11.47', 1.78km/140m, 7 min]* until you reach another T *[9. 06.57'/11.34', 1.97km/190m, 7 min].*

Turn right past a small farmhouse, and follow the path round to the left past a raised well. Continue past more farm buildings until the path emerges on to a track *[10. 06.66'/11.32', 2.14km/170m, 6 min].* Turn right, and follow the track until it meets the concrete road from Skala Polichnitou to Skamnioudi *[11. 07.04'/11.48', 2.92km/780m, 9 min].*

Go ahead along the road until a concrete bridge crosses a stream. On the far side of the bridge a track leads off to the left *[12. 07.16'/11.63', 3.22km/300m, 4 min].* Take it, and follow it along the river-bank down to the shore of the Gulf of Kalloni. Straight ahead across the gulf is the village of Parakoila. (in the ruins of the Turkish settlement near Parakoila - to the left of the village as you look across - is the remains of a mosque with the only complete minaret left on Lesvos – to visit it see Walk 18) *[13. 07.57'/11.39', 4.12km/900m, 12 min].*
Turn right and walk along to the fishing harbour of Skamnioudi. There are two tavernas here where you can take a break before starting the return leg of the walk *[14. 07.73'/12.28', 5.52km/1.40km, 17 min].*

Continue north out of the harbour (with the sea on your left). After about 500 metres the track rises to the right to run above a low earth cliff *[15. 07.95'/12.43', 5.99km/470m, 6 min].* If you leave the track here, tide and wind permitting, and continue along the stony beach, you will see remains of the masonry of ancient Pyrra, one of the six founding city states of Lesvos, protruding from the cliff. The remains of the city, many of them now under the sea, extend from Skamnioudi to Achladeri, seven kilometres to the north-east.

The track descends to rejoin the beach; to the right is the Alikoudi lake (Αλικούδι), a large salty lagoon, dry in summer, but at other seasons a magnet for flamingos and other wading birds.

Ignore the first track to the right after the lagoon; continue to the second and turn right *[16. 07.83'/13.33', 7.38km/1.39km, 20 min]*.

Walk up to the concrete road, and cross it to the track opposite (there is a spring and water-trough on the left) *[17. 07.72'/13.35', 7.60km/220m, 4 min]*. Follow this track uphill, ignoring side tracks, until it goes sharply to the left *[18. 07.46'/13.18', 8.20km/600m, 8 min]*. Take the footpath leading ahead to the right: it goes through overgrown holly-oak and olive groves to join the end of a narrow track. Ignore the field entrance to the right and continue to a T-junction with a broad kalderimi *[19. 07.23'/12.97', 8.76km/560m, 9 min]*.

To see what are reputed to be the oldest olive trees on Lesvos, turn right for a short distance; otherwise turn left uphill.

Follow the track, much of it on well-preserved kalderimi, as it undulates up and down (but mostly up, often steeply). Ignore all crossings and side tracks. About a hundred metres after it finally becomes concrete, running between stone walls, look for a path to the right *[20. 06.62'/12.89', 9.98km/1.22km, 16 min]*.

Take this. You will soon see ruined buildings on the right – go beyond them, through an entrance, and back down past the buildings to the bottom of the field, where there is an underground spring in a chamber cut into the rock, with a channel feeding a cistern *[21. 06.62'/12.84', 10.00km/20m, 4 min]*.

Then return to the path (it becomes a track almost immediately) and continue past a farm to its junction with a road *[22. 06.57'/12.80', 10.20km/200m, 4 min]*. Turn right downhill for 300 metres, then left along a track to the left of a barn *[23. 06.63'/12.60', 10.50km/300m, 4 min]*. Pass a chapel on the right, and come to another road *[24. 06.23'/12.74', 11.30km/800m, 12 min]*.

Cross to the track opposite, and go downhill to cross a bridge over a stream. Turn right at the T-junction immediately afterwards *[25. 06.10'/12.71', 11.59km/290m, 8 min]*, and go up past a large farm building and pond. When the main track bends sharp left uphill, continue ahead *[26. 06.00'/12.50', 11.89km/300m, 5 min]*, and bear right across open ground. Follow the faint track across the plateau; it bends right and leads downhill on loose stone, with greenhouses and the Lisvori thermal baths below and ahead, to end at the opening to a field *[27. 06.04'/12.30', 12.29km/400m, 5 min]*.

Go into the field and sharp left along its edge. At the end of the field cross the fence a few metres above its bottom corner and continue through the next field to the olive grove ahead. Then go downhill to a concrete bridge which joins the road opposite the baths, and turn right for a few metres to complete your walk *[28. 06.08'/12.08', 12.69km/400m, 7 min]*.

Hot Springs and Holy Places around Polichnitos

12

Total distance 8 kilometres

 Walking time 2½ hours

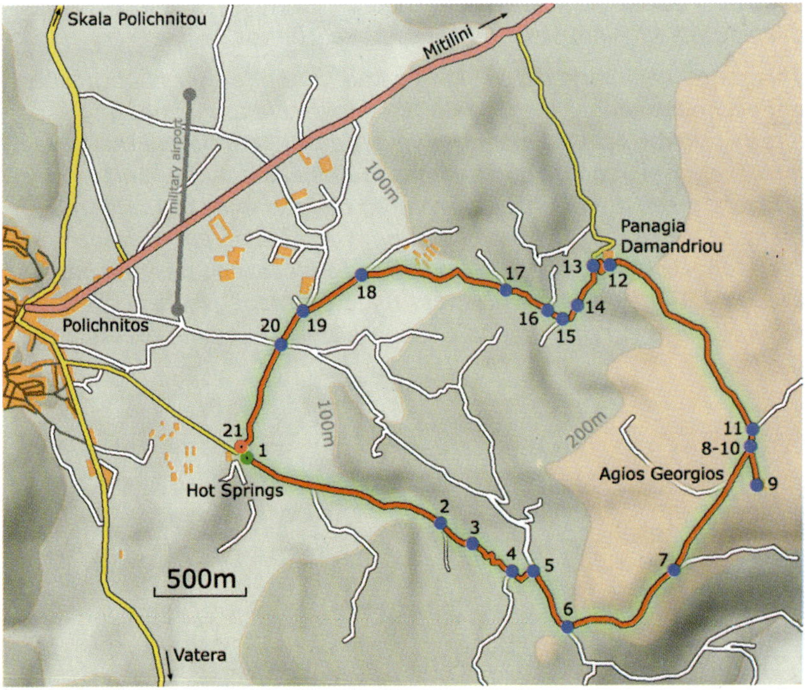

The Thermal Baths of Polichnitos are built over the hottest springs on Lesvos, the water from some of which reaches temperatures close to boiling, up to 92°C. The water is especially rich in minerals, including, according to the Thermal Baths website, 'carbonic acid, chloride and sulphate, sodium and calcium salts, free carbon dioxide, iron, magnesium and manganese compounds, as well as oxygen and traces of iodine and bromium'. These, and the algae which they nourish, have stained the steaming banks of the surrounding streams in rich reddish-browns and vivid greens.

This walk starts from the Thermal Baths and leads you along old kalderimi and up to one of the few level plateaux in Lesvos, at an altitude of over 200 metres. Here you will find Agios Georgios, once a small monastery, a dependency (metochi) of Panagia Damandriou, and now a beautiful and isolated place of pilgrimage and retreat. It continues to Panagia Damandriou, originally a Byzantine foundation, rebuilt, probably in the 17th century, after a long period of abandonment. After passing through more olive groves it brings you, with our apologies, back to the 21st century in the form of the dilapidated agri-industrial outskirts of Polichnitos.

This route was marked and sign-posted by the former Municipality of Polichnitos, under the EC LEADER+ initiative to encourage alternative forms of tourism. However, as we mention in the introduction, in common with other routes across the island, budgetary constraints have prevented maintenance of the signs, many of which, at the time of writing, were falling into disrepair. We therefore have not mentioned them in the following descriptions, though you may well come across fingerposts, as well as yellow rectangular and red diamond or square trekking trail markers along the way.

To reach the Thermal Baths take the Vatera road out of Polichnitos, and turn left, signposted to the Thermal Baths, shortly after passing a parking area on the left and a filling station on the right. The baths are just over 1 kilometre along this road, on the right immediately after a large military base.

Start from the parking area at the hot springs *[1. 39°04.47′/26°11.99′]*. Walk along the short stretch of paved road heading away from the army base and go uphill on a concrete track. Where the track divides keep on the left fork going ahead. The track becomes narrower and more overgrown: where a path leads off to the right across a stream go straight ahead on a kalderimi footpath *[2. 04.32′/12.66′, 940m, 12 min]*.

Follow this path, which can be overgrown in places. It leads gently uphill, and across a rocky outcrop. Follow the path as it leads down to the right *[3. 04.26′/12.78′, 1.15km/210m, 8 min]*, and then winds uphill on kaldermi – in places there are steps edged with retaining lengths of timber. It leads round sharp left and runs alongside a fence. This stretch is narrow and rocky, and finally rises up a bank to meet a track *[4. 04.18′/12.93′, 1.39km/240m, 10 min]*.

Turn left on to the track and stay with it when it takes an almost

right-angle left-hand bend and leads uphill, ignoring the path ahead. When you come to a T-junction turn right *[5. 04.19'/13.02', 1.54km/210m, 5 min]*.

Carry on uphill. Just before the brow of the hill take the concrete track going uphill to the left *[6. 04.02'/13.15', 1.91km/370m, 5 min]*.

The track climbs steadily – far over to the right you will begin to catch glimpses of the sea near Vatera.

When it forks keep left and continue to climb *[7. 04.18'/13.54', 2.61km/700m, 12 min]*. You climb out of the olive groves and emerge on to a wide plateau dotted with pines, holly oak, and the occasional oak tree. Over to your right there are the white walls enclosing the oasis of Agios Georgios. Walk on to the next junction and turn right *[8. 04.51'/13.83', 3.35km/740m, 10 min]*.

Walk along to Agios Georgios *[9. 04.41'/13.87', 3.52km/170m, 3 min]*. This is approximately the half-way point of your walk (and the end of any significant climbing!), and you can take a well-earned break in the shady gardens.

Return to the junction *[10. 04.51'/13.83', 3.69km/170m, 3 min]* and go straight ahead. At the next cross-track turn left *[11. 04.56'/13.85', 3.79km/100m, 2 min]*.

Follow this track as it heads down off the plateau. Across the valley ahead Polichnitos's neighbour, the hill-village of Lisvori, comes into view, with the Gulf of Kalloni beyond. Continue down, ignoring all side-tracks, until after sharp left and right bends you come on to the concrete forecourt of the monastery of Panagia Damandriou *[12. 05.05'/13.29', 5.18km/1.39km, 25 min]*.

From the monastery, walk downhill on the concrete road until the first right-hand bend, then take the path leading ahead on the left of the turn *[13. 05.03'/13.26', 5.25km/70m, 2 min]*. It widens, leading steeply downhill. When it levels out, fork right on to a narrow path leading along a terrace. *[14. 04.90'/13.17', 5.51km/260m, 5 min]*.

The path bends to the right and winds steeply downhill on solid rock. At the bottom turn right alongside a stream *[15. 04.88'/13.13', 5.58km/70m, 7 min]*. Follow round across a wooden bridge and up to meet a track *[16. 04.90'/13.08', 5.66km/80m, 4 min]*.

Turn left and follow the track down through olive groves until it swings to the right over a small ridge *[17. 04.96'/12.91', 5.87km/210m, 6 min]*. Ignore the path leading ahead; instead go left and immediately right. This path soon becomes a track, with a stream to the left. Follow it through olive groves, ignoring side turnings. It swings left before a group of large factory-farm buildings, and leads on through the agri-industry area on the edge of Polichnitos to a T-junction *[18. 05.00'/12.38', 6.63km/760m, 15 min]*.

Turn left, and at the next crossing turn left again, staying on the main track *[19. 04.90'/12.14', 7.03km/400m, 6 min]*. Go straight ahead at the next *[20. 04.82'/12.08', 7.20km/170m, 4 min]*, and continue until you meet the asphalt road. Then turn left and walk the final few metres back to the hot springs car park *[21. 04.47'/11.99', 7.92km/720m, 10 min]*.

Vrisa, Vatera, and Paleopirgos

13

Total distance 11 kilometres

 Walking time 3 hours

This varied walk brings together many of the most interesting and attractive features of southern Lesvos. It starts and finishes with an opportunity to explore the tiny traditional town of Vrisa, which has a population of only 800, but which is home to a fascinating natural history museum (featured in the 2010 BBCtv documentary 'Aristotle's Lagoon'). Opened in 1999, it is part of Athens University Museum of Paleontology and Geology and contains fossils of elephants and antelopes dating from two million years ago, when

Lesvos was still joined to Asia Minor and had a climate similar to today's African savannah.

You then climb out of the town over the ridge of hills that separates it from the coast (the only significant climb of the walk!), and descend through olive groves and pine woods, with beautiful sea views on the way, to the wide, six-kilometre stretch of south-facing sand that is Vatera beach.

After a walk along the beach (and possibly a swim), you turn inland again along the bank of the reedy Almiropotamos (Αλμυροπόταμος – 'Salty river'). This is a favourite area for bird-watchers: many waders and other water-birds, together with a variety of raptors and other birds, feed and nest here.

The walk finally returns through olive-groves to Vrisa, on the way visiting Paleopirgos (Παλιόπυργος – Ancient tower). This watch-tower, on a mound near Vrisa which dominates the river valley down to the sea, is also known as the Gatelouzo Tower, after the Genoese dynasty that ruled the island in the 14th and 15th centuries before being ousted by the Ottomans. It is probable, however, that an earlier tower preceded their rule, built to protect the 'new' Vrisa after the previous coastal settlement was destroyed by Seljuk raiders in 1080AD.

Vrisa is situated beside the main road from Polichnitos to Vatera, about 5km south of Polichnitos. It is an old-fashioned Greek island

town, *full of narrow winding streets where it is easy to get lost and very difficult to park. We recommend that you enter from the southern end, taking the street next to the EKO filling station. If you then take the third street to the left, you should find parking space where it widens out after the first narrow, downhill, fifty metres. Walk back up to the main street and turn left to reach the beginning of the walk – you will pass the museum a few metres downhill to the left on the corner of a small square.*

The walk starts in the centre of Vrisa, in the small square on the main street outside the ΟΥΖΕΡΙ Ο ΠΛΑΤΑΝΟΣ, under the large plane tree that gives the ouzeri its name *[1. 39°02.41′/026°12.00′]*. Walk up the street leading away from the square (8th October – there is a faded enamel sign on the wall opposite the ouzeri; ΟΔΟΣ 8ΗΣ ΟΚ/ΒΡΙΟ – a / in a Greek word indicates the missing letters in an abbreviation).

Ignore all side turnings, but carry on slightly uphill until the street bends to the right and then comes to a T-junction, where it turns sharp right uphill *[2. 02.32′/12.12′, 210m, 4 min]*. Turn left here towards a track, but immediately go right again on an impossibly steep concrete street (any steeper and it would be a cliff!). It winds uphill out of the town, and becomes a track leading through farmland to a crossing *[3. 02.18′/12.27′, 610m/400m, 10 min]*.

Go straight ahead, ignore a track leading back to the right, and come to a T-junction, where you turn right *[4. 02.12′/12.31′, 750m/140m, 3 min]*. Follow this track as far as the next junction, and then turn left downhill *[5. 01.96′/12.11′, 1.14km/390m, 5 min]*.

Go downhill through olive groves and pine trees. Ignore a track leading off to the left, and at the fork shortly afterwards keep right downhill *[6. 01.62'/12.12', 1.78km/640m, 16 min]*.

Along this stretch the track is sunk deep between high earth banks, and is very rough in places. It eventually leads under the stone arch of a road bridge and comes to a T-junction *[7. 01.37'/12.03', 2.31km/530m, 10 min]*.

Turn left on to the concrete road (there is a modern ornamental well on your left at the junction). Ignore two junctions to the right, keeping ahead but bearing slightly left at each, and continue until you come out on the asphalt road behind Vatera beach *[8. 01.17'/12.03', 2.72km/410m, 6 min]*.

Cross the road and turn right. Walk along the sandy beach (the sand is soft and hard work for walking, so you may prefer to stay on the road). Pause for a swim and/or refreshments at one of the beach tavernas if you wish, and when you are ready go on until you reach the last street-light (the asphalt also ends here) *[9. 01.06'/10.98', 4.29km/1.57km, 20 min]*.

Follow the dirt road round to the right alongside the Almiropotamos (literally 'salty river') and continue until you reach a bridge *[10. 01.24'/10.83', 4.73km/440m, 7 min]*. Turn left to cross the river, then right along the opposite bank.

(If you turn left here and follow the road you will, after 2½km, arrive at Cape Fokas. There is a charming fishing harbour here, and a popular fish taverna. There are the remains of an ancient temple

of Dionysos on the cape, as well as the foundations of an early Christian basilica, and on the way you will pass an old stone well and small cistern known as Achilles' Well. The ancient town of Vrisa was also in this area, until the need to protect themselves against marauders from the sea drove its inhabitants inland.)

Follow the track along the river-bank as far as the next bridge. Look out for your first views of Paleopirgos in the distance ahead of you. This reedy, watery area is where the bird-watchers among you will get delayed! Turn left at the bridge *[11. 02.06'/10.49', 6.43km/1.70km, 22 min]* and walk away from the river through olive groves until you reach an off-set crossing *[12. 02.16'/10.34', 6.74km/310m, 5 min]*.

Turn right, and continue through the olive groves to the next T-junction *[13. 02.53'/10.45', 7.63km/890m, 10 min]*. Turn right here along a lesser track, which leads down to and across the river at a ford.

Cross the river (there may be stepping stones, but you should be prepared for wet feet), and on reaching the other side turn left on the track along the bank *[14. 02.53'/10.57', 7.82km/190m, 5 min]*. At the next junction turn right *[15. 02.61'/10.63', 7.99km/170m, 5 min]* and walk gently uphill.

Paleopirgos is now on the mound ahead of you to the left; to reach it take the track uphill to the left at the next junction *[16. 02.69'/10.89', 8.72km/730m, 10 min]*. There should be a sign at the junction, but the track soon ends and you will have to find your own way through two small fields to reach the tower itself *[17. 02.67'/10.79', 8.90km/180m, 6 min]*.

Retrace your steps down the mound and turn left on to the main track. Walk on to a T-junction and turn right *[18. 02.64'/11.81', 10.58km/1.68km, 20 min]*. Then continue to the main road and go straight across into the lane opposite *[19. 02.55'/11.86', 10.76km/180m, 3 min]*.

Walk along the lane, crossing a stream bed. It enters Vrisa and leads past the church of Agia Marina (Αγ Μαρίνα) before ending at the main street *[20. 02.39'/11.97', 11.09km/330m, 5 min]*. Turn left and walk down the main street to return to your starting point *[21. 02.41'/12.00', 11.13km/40m, 1 min]*.

From Melinta to Panagia Krifti and Paleochori

14

Total distance 10 kilometres

 Walking time 3½ hours

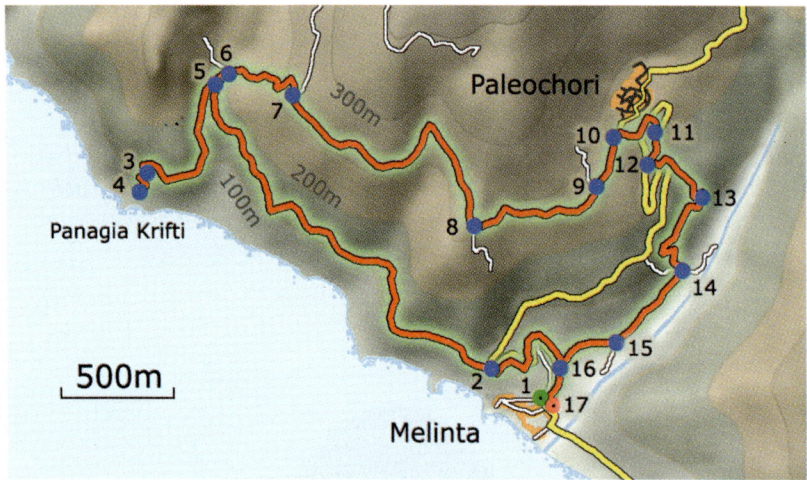

This walk takes you from the small and little-known beach resort of Melinta (Μελίντα) along the stunning rugged coastline of south-east Lesvos to the 'secret' cave church of Panagia Krifti (Παναγία Κρυφτή), almost hidden under the cliffs in a remote cove. You then climb through olive groves on a winding footpath (μονοπάτι) before returning via the old traditional village of Paleochori (Παλαιοχωρι) and a tranquil river valley.

This is a beautiful, but in places strenuous walk, with some very steep ascents and descents. Fortunately the most strenuous stretch is through olive groves, where there is ample shade at any time of year.

The easiest way to reach Melinta is via Plomari. Take the turning to Gera and Plomari off the Mitilini – Kalloni road 10km from Mitilini. Plomari is a further 28km from this junction. From Plomari continue along the coast road for another 6km to reach Melinda.

The walk starts from the T-junction in Melinta where the main road turns right, signposted to Paleochori. Turn left and park in the paved street which leads down to the resort.

From the start *[1. 38°59.25'/26°18.88']* walk uphill on the tarmac road round left- and right- hand hairpin bends, ignoring tracks off to the left, until you reach the second right-hand hairpin bend. A dirt road leads off to the left along the coast at the apex of the bend *[2. 59.33'/18.71', 750m, 10 min]. (You will hate us for this beginning, but may thank us later when at the end of your walk you re-emerge on the road less than 200 metres uphill from your parking place!)*

Follow the dirt road. It climbs along the coastline high above the sea, with spectacular views of the cliffs and tiny, inaccessible beaches below. On clear days you can see across to the island of Chios, nearly 50 kilometres to the south-west, and, closer and further east, the mainland of Turkey.

The road eventually bends to the right and leads down around the end of a valley. It passes a white-washed water-fountain and trough

on the right, and continues downhill, becoming narrower, rougher and steeper until it comes to an end high above a rocky cove [3. 59.78'/17.65', 3.69km/2.94km, 45 min].

Look for a small path leading down to the right (not the apparent path ahead). Follow it downhill with great care – it is extremely steep, with a loose stony surface. When it is joined by a path coming downhill from the opposite direction, turn right, and go on down. As you wind down you will begin to catch glimpses of the tiled roof of the entrance to Panagia Krifti, and its tiny landing-stage. For the final few metres of the descent there is a blue-painted handrail leading to a paved terrace [4. 59.74'/17.61', 3.76km/70m, 10 min].

The chapel itself is in a natural cave behind the entrance portico (Krifti – Κρυφτή means hidden or secret – the legend is that a woman hid her young daughter in the cave to prevent her being taken by the Ottoman occupiers for their harems). Steps lead on down to the landing-stage, and there is also a hot spring here, which feeds a small bath at a constant temperature of 70°C.

Climb back up to the track and return to the white water-fountain

[5. 39°00.00'/26°17.89', 4.67km/910m, 20 min]. Look for a small path leading uphill to the right of the fountain, and follow it up through olive groves to a chapel. It passes in front of the chapel and then divides *[6. 00.02'/17.92', 4.70km/30m, 8 min].*

Go right and follow the path along immediately above the chapel. It leads uphill along the edge of a valley, then bends down to the right to cross a stream. It climbs again, and winds uphill through the olives. When you reach an small open area ahead of you to the left, follow the path round sharp right and continue to climb. Go on steeply uphill, always taking the clearest path. Just when you begin to think the climb will never end, the path finally emerges on to a track *[7. 38°59.96'/26°18.13', 5.05km/350m, 25 min].*

Turn right and follow track round the end of a valley. Pass a chapel above you on the left, and at the next junction keep left on the main track *[8. 59.67'/18.66', 6.33km/1.28km, 15 min].* When you come to a fork, where a concrete track leads left and right, keep right, continuing downhill *[9. 59.77'/19.05', 6.97km/640m, 11 min].*

The hill village of Paleochori comes into sight ahead of you: at the next junction ignore the small track leading back downhill to the right, but continue for a few more metres to reach a parking area where the asphalt road enters the village *[10. 59.89'/19.11', 7.21km/240m, 5 min].*

To explore the narrow streets and the square of this lovely traditional village, go straight ahead. Although much of the street is barely one car wide, and there are several sharp corners, this is a main road, and there are frequent nose to nose confrontations. Take extra care not to become the filling in a sandwich!

To continue the walk, turn right from the parking area and walk down the road. You pass a modern olive press on the left, and a much older, though still operational, one on the right. Follow the road round to the right, and almost immediately after the turn take a kalderimi downhill to the left *[11. 59.90'/19.25', 7.50km/290m, 7 min].*

Follow the path down; it varies between kalderimi, rough narrow loose stone, and earth path through olives. When it meets a track turn left and continue downhill (a short distance uphill to the right you will see the main road) *[12. 59.82'/19.23', 7.75km/250m, 6 min].*

The track soon ends. Go on down the path, passing a spring on the left, and carry straight on down until the path meets another track. Turn right here *[13. 59.76'/19.43', 8.22km/470m, 15 min]*, and follow the track as it leads along the side of the valley and then zig-zags down to a staggered crossing *[14. 59.58'/19.36', 8.84km/620m, 17 min]*.

Turn right, and immediately right again, and walk along the level track with a river on your left (the river is hardly visible from the track, but depending on the time of year you may hear the sound of flowing water). You pass a small-holding and cottage on the left, and at the next fork keep right *[15. 59.40'/19.11', 9.32km/480m, 10 min]*.

The track ends at the main road *[16. 59.34'/18.92', 9.64km/320m, 4 min]*. Turn left on to the road and walk downhill to the junction to complete your walk *[17. 59.25'/18.88', 9.81km/170m, 4 min]*.

Along the Gulf of Gera
from Avlonas to Katsinia

15

Total distance 7¼ kilometres

 Walking time 2¼ hours

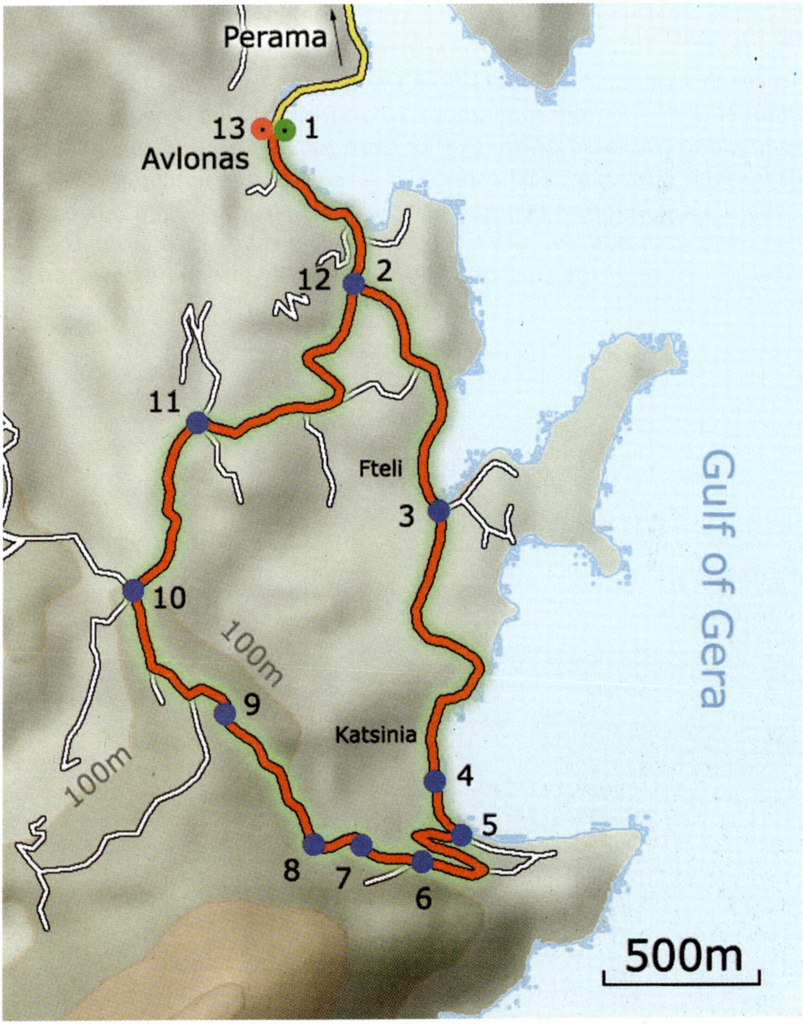

On the western shore of the Gulf of Gera, near its mouth, there are a series of beautiful bays, backed by olive groves, with tranquil unpopulated beaches which are ideal for swimming and picnicking. This relatively short and easy walk (there is only one significant climb) takes you past some of them, before heading into the hills through olive groves to return along a high ridge. It gives you ample time for a break on a beach either shortly before the half-way point or towards the end, and you can round it off with lunch at the taverna in Avlonas itself, or in one of the other villages further up the gulf.

To reach Avlonas (Αύλωνας) take the turning to Plomari off the main Mitilini – Kalloni road about 10km from Mitilini. Follow the road along the head of the Gulf of Gera for 2.7km, and turn left to Perama (Πέραμα). (Be especially careful at this junction; it is immediately before a blind bend on a hill. Drivers coming down can't see you, and you can't see them.) The road leads along the western shore of the Gulf of Gera, through Perama, which was once

*home to a flourishing leather industry, the largest in the Balkans,
the disused shells of whose tanneries now line the roadside. It
continues through Marmaro (Μάρμαρο) and Pirgi (Πύργοι) to
Avlonas. The road is narrow, and it is difficult to find a safe place
to park in Avlonas itself: we recommend that you continue through
the village down to the shore, where there is ample space. We start
the walk here, on the beach road just after it crosses a stream bed,
where a track goes off to the right.*

From the start *[1. 39°00.60'/26°31.86']*, carry on along the
concrete road with the sea on your left. The concrete ends after
a few metres, and a dirt road continues over a small headland
before bending right and heading inland. Follow it, ignoring the
track leading ahead around the edge of the bay. A short distance
further on, where a concrete track goes ahead up a steep hill,
bear left. (You will come down the concrete track on your return.)
[2. 00.35'/32.03', 610m, 10 min].

The track leads up to cross the next headland: at the brow of the
hill ignore the track to the right, but continue downhill back to the
sea at Fteli (Φτέλι) beach, and then at the next junction turn right

away from the coast again *[3. 38°59.97'/26°32.22', 1.52km/910m, 15 min]*.

Walk on through olive groves, ignoring tracks off to the left and right. The track climbs gently, and then descends again to Katsinia (Κατσίνια). This is an idyllic bay, with a few fishermen's cottages, and their boats drawn up on the beach – an ideal spot for a break and a swim.

Walk along to a gate at the far end of the beach *[4. 59.52'/32.21', 2.59km/1.07km, 20 min]*. Go round the end of the gate (it is simply there to bar the way to vehicles), continue on the track to the next junction, and bend round uphill to the right *[5. 59.42'/32.27', 2.83km/240m, 3 min]*. In spring and early summer you may find several varieties of orchid and other wild flowers here.

Zig-zag uphill, keeping to the main track, and ignoring a path off to the right, until you reach a fork *[6. 59.38'/32.18', 3.45km/620m, 12 min]*. Take the track to the right, which starts level, and then climbs gently, until it ends at a large old olive tree. Leaving the tree on your left, go down to the top of a terrace, then bear left

up to a gap in the terrace wall ahead of you [7. 59.40'/32.05', 3.65km/200m, 5 min].

Go up through the gap into an olive grove, with a deep valley a short distance over to your right. Go straight ahead for a few metres to find the beginning of a small path, which bears up left before leading along above the valley until it reaches an old stone hut at the end of a track [8. 59.40'/31.94', 3.83km/180m, 8 min].

Follow the track uphill across the end of the valley. You come to a staggered junction, with tracks going off to the left and right. Ignore these, but stay on the main track, bearing left uphill, until you reach a fenced olive grove on the right, with a small cottage and barbecue. There is a track leading off downhill immediately beyond this: ignore it [9. 59.63'/31.74', 4.37km/540m, 10 min].

Continue over the brow of the hill to a T-junction. Turn right downhill – the track runs just below the ridge and there are stupendous views on the left, south-west through the densely-wooded valley towards the coast. Follow the track until you come to a crossing, where there is a water-fountain, with a roofed shelter alongside, and a small stone farm building in the field behind [10. 59.83'/31.53', 4.93km/560m, 10 min].

Turn right, and wind downhill, ignoring side tracks. The track you are on re-enters olive groves and reaches a junction [11. 39°00.12'/26°31.68', 5.59km/660m, 10 min]. Turn right and climb briefly as the track goes over a ridge, then follow it downhill towards the bottom of the valley. At the bottom of the hill another track comes in from the right: ignore it and rise again, bearing left round the end of the hill before descending again as the bay of Avlonas comes into sight ahead.

Keep on this track, ignoring side turnings. It bends to the left and climbs briefly once more, before descending steeply on concrete to a junction at the bottom of the hill [12. 00.35'/32.03', 6.58km/990m, 15 min].

This was point 2 on your outbound route: go straight ahead, then bear left and follow the coast back to your starting point [13. 00.60'/31.86', 7.24km/660m, 10 min].

From Skala Kallonis through the salt-flats

16

Total distance 10 kilometres

 Walking time 2¾ hours

Skala Kallonis (Σκάλα Καλλονής) is a flourishing fishing village, and together with Molivos, Petra and Anaxos, one of the main holiday resorts of Lesvos. Its south-facing position at the head of the Gulf of Kalloni gives it a warm, shallow sea, sandy beaches, and plentiful fish. It is surrounded by low-lying salt flats and lagoons, and fertile alluvial plains, which make it particularly attractive to resident and migratory sea-birds and waders, and to the many bird-watchers who flock here each year in the hope of seeing them. The village is also famous for its mascot non-migratory one-legged pelican, which

you may well see patrolling the harbour.

On this walk, at any time of year, you are likely to see herons, egrets, and flamingos, as well as other smaller and migratory water-birds. It leads you from Skala Kallonis along the banks of the river Tsianas (Τσιανάς), and on to a long stretch of sandy beach ideal for swimming. It then turns inland near the larger of the two salt-works on the gulf (which produces up to 40,000 tonnes of sea salt per year from its 2.5 sq km of salt-pans) and returns through the varied agricultural countryside via the villages of Keramio (Κεράμιο) and Papiana (Παπιανά).

To reach Skala Kallonis take the road south from Kalloni (a continuation of the main street) towards Parakoila, Agra, and Mesopotos, and look for the signed turning to the left after about 2.5km. This road will lead you directly in to Skala Kallonis and the parking area at the fishing harbour. The walk starts by the harbour side, at the taverna-lined square in the centre of the village.

Note that this walk includes two river crossings. Both crossings have a firm concrete track across the river-bed, and from spring

to autumn there will usually be little or no water in the river, so you should have no problems. If there is too much water for a safe crossing, you can either continue to the road bridge and cross there (though this will add over six kilometres to the total distance of the walk), or shorten the walk by staying on the Skala Kallonis side of the river and going directly from point 5 to point 12 before continuing from there. This is of course also an option if you would prefer a shorter circular walk leaving out the beach and salt-pans.

From the starting point *[1. 39°12.34'/026°12.64']* walk east along the water-front road, with the sea on your right. Take the second street leading inland to your left *[2. 12.33'/12.70', 80m, 2 min]*, and at the next, six-way junction, go ahead, bearing slightly right, until you reach a T-junction *[3. 12.40'/12.74', 220m/140m, 2 min]*.

Turn right on to an asphalt road, and when it bends round to the left go straight on a dirt road. Pass a large exotic pink structure (an open-air night-club) on your left, and continue until the road turns left along a river-bank *[4. 12.31'/13.15', 860m/640m, 10 min]*.

Follow the road alongside the river until you reach the first crossing

point *[5. 12.66'/13.38', 1.60km/740m, 11 min]*. Cross here – a track leads diagonally back down the river bank, then across a concrete strip on the river bed, and diagonally up the opposite side to another dirt road *[6. 12.64'/13.40', 1.65km/50m, 3 min]*.

Turn right on to the road, and walk down the opposite bank of the river until the road bends away to the left. Keep ahead along a path for a few metres until you come to a gate in a fence *[7. 12.26'/13.23', 2.44km/790m, 10 min]*.

Go through the gate, and continue along the river-bank until you reach its mouth, then turn left along the beach. Walk along the beach – there may be several easily passable brushwood barriers and fences across the beach on this stretch - with the white salt-mountain that marks the Kalloni salt works ahead of you. You will also see the remains of the jetty where the salt used to be loaded on to barges to be taken to the harbour of Skala Polichnitou for transfer to larger sea-going ships: now it is all trucked through the hills to the port of Petra in the north of the island.

When you reach a shack housing a seasonal beach café *[8. 12.44'/14.69', 4.84km/2.40km, 50 min]* go out through its entrance on to a track and straight ahead until you reach an asphalt road. Continue ahead, with the salt pans on your right, for about a kilometre, until the road bends sharp right just after a fenced compound (housing a sewage farm) on the left.

Take the track that leads off to the left at the apex of the bend [9. 12.83'/14.32', 5.89km/1.05km, 13 min]. It leads alongside a water channel, and at the end bends to the right. Continue to follow this track past a junction to the right [10. 12.99'/14.07', 6.41km/520m, 7 min], and briefly alongside a short air-strip, where it bends to the left and right and goes on to emerge finally on an asphalt road alongside the river [11. 13.26'/13.40', 7.56km/1.15km, 20 min]. (The large industrial buildings behind trees on your left at this point are the island's largest and most modern abattoirs.)

Cross the road and take the track down the river bank. A concrete strip leads across the river, and another track leads up the opposite bank a few metres down-stream. When you reach the dirt road go down the track directly opposite [12. 13.26'/13.35', 7.61km/50m, 3 min].

Walk along between olive groves, and at the first crossing turn left [13. 13.32'/13.18', 7.90km/290m, 4 min].

At the next junction, ignore the track to the left [14. 13.12'/12.99', 8.36km/460m, 6 min]. The main track bears right, and immediately comes to a second junction at a triangle. Keep right here, and then quickly bear left at a fork [15. 13.14'/12.94', 8.01km/110m, 4 min].

Go on along this track until you reach a T-junction. Turn left here towards the village of Keramio (Κεράμιο) [16. 13.16'/12.70', 8.36km/350m, 4 min]. The track enters the village and comes to a T-junction with an asphalt road [17. 12.94'/12.50', 8.88km/520m, 6 min]. Turn left and walk along the road, passing the village school on your left.

At the cross-roads a little further on follow the main road round to the right, and at the next fork (where both roads are sign-posted to Skala Kallonis) keep straight ahead. The road now bends to the left in front of a church, and then to the right – you are now in Papiana (Παπιανά).

Stay on the main street winding through the village until, with a bus stop on the left and a football pitch on the right, it enters the outskirts of Skala Kallonis and leads you back to the square, where you can take your pick of the tavernas for a well-earned meal [18. 12.34'/12.64', 10.06km/1.18km, 17 min].

Pilgrims' Way – Leimonos and its Dependencies

17

Total distance 5¾ kilometres

Walking time 2 hours

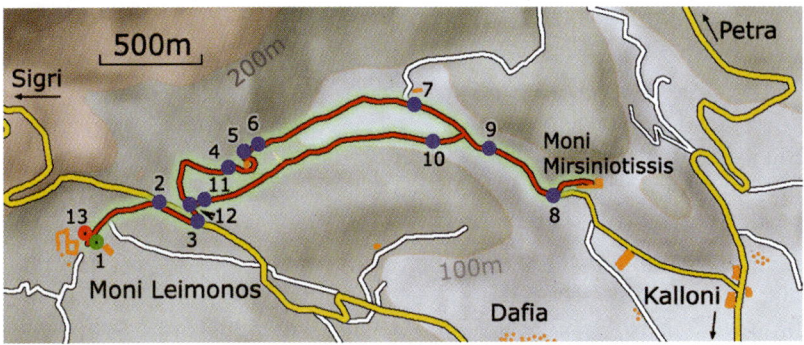

Leimonos Monastery and Myrsiniotissis Convent were both re-established in the 1520s on the ruins of earlier Byzantine foundations by John Agallianos, on whose family estates the sites were situated. He was later canonised as St Ignatios, and Leimonos is dedicated to him. The monasteries became centres of education and local solidarity throughout the centuries of Ottoman rule: monks from Leimonos took part in the final campaign against the occupiers in 1912.

Over the centuries eight further monasteries dependent on Leimonos (in Greek called metochi - μετόχη) have been established on Lesvos; in addition to Myrsiniotissis this walk visits two of the nearest and most recent, and returns along the original cobbled road (kalderimi) linking the original foundations.

Be sure to allow time to visit Leimonos and Myrsiniotissis as well as enjoying your walk. As well as providing a picture of Orthodox monastic life Leimonos in particular has an interesting museum as well as many beautiful and unexpected features, not least the families of peacocks that patrol its precincts. There is a taverna in the parking area with drinks and simple meals.

Leimonos is about 4½ kilometres from Kalloni on the road towards Vatoussa and Antissa, in a valley down to the right of the road. There is ample parking space directly outside the monastery.

Start from the parking area in front of the main gate of the monastery *[1. 39°14.88'/26°10.40']* and walk back up the access road past some of the many chapels built in recent years with donations from the faithful. At the junction with the main road   *[2. 14.98'/10.64', 420m, 5 min],* turn right, and walk along the road, with views to the left across the valley to the next two monasteries on your route.

At the next junction on the left, take the track running sharply back down the hillside *[3. 14.93'/10.77', 630m/210m, 5 min].* At the bottom of the hill it bends right across a stream and passes a modern chapel on the right. At the fork shortly after this keep right on the main lower track.

Continue until you see a chapel on a left-hand bend at the brow of a hill: immediately before this take the rough track down to the right *[4. 15.07'/10.87', 1.20km/570m, 20 min],* leading to the small, recently-built (some of the detailing remains unfinished), metochi of St Nikolaos Planas *[5. 15.06'/10.94', 1.30km/100m, 5 min].* At the time of writing the buildings were unoccupied and kept locked, but by peering through the rails of the entrance gate you can get a glimpse of the charming inner courtyard. The monastery is built on the site of an old water-mill ('Sotiri's Mill'), whose masonry and water channels are still visible above and below the later buildings.

Cross the channel to the right of the monastery (there is a half-

metre drop on the far side), follow round the building and take the path leading back up to the track *[6. 15.09'/10.93', 1.39km/90m, 5 min]*. Turn right and continue downhill and then through level farmland until you reach the next junction *[7. 15.22'/11.50', 2.32km/930m, 15 min]*. The walk continues on the track ahead, which bears slightly to the right. The large uncompleted building on the junction is the metochi of Christ of the Nuns; its entrance lies few metres off the track leading uphill to the left.

Restoration and rebuilding has been going on here for a number of years. The gates may be locked, but if not it is worth exploring inside. The tiny original monastery church remains, replaced by a modern building alongside. The full length of the upper side of the quadrangle forms an impressive refectory, while modern paved cloisters are being built below the lower, right-hand side, extending round to the far side. Monastic cells and guest rooms can be seen taking shape above.

Continue along the main track. It leads into pine forest, passing a small white chapel above to the left. At the next junction it becomes a concrete road *[8. 14.99'/11.95', 3.14km/820m, 10 min]*.

The wide concrete spur up to the left leads to Myrsiniotissis Convent, which is still occupied by a few elderly nuns. It is open to visitors daily, except between 1 and 3pm. Built into a south-facing hillside, it is a beautifully sheltered, flower-filled place, and there are shady spots outside for your half-way break.

Then return to the junction, and retrace your steps. After re-entering the pine forest and passing the chapel, now on the right, look out for blue and red marks on rocks at the side of the track on the left. *[9. 15.11'/11.73', 3.59km/450m, 10 min].*

Take the path that, after a steep, rocky start, bends to the right and runs parallel to the track above, descending gradually towards the bottom of the valley, with blue markers at intervals. It eventually turns sharp left and crosses a stream, with the ruined masonry of an old stone bridge on the left. It then rises on a soft path through the forest and shortly becomes a kalderimi.

Follow the kalderimi along the opposite side of the valley to your outbound route, passing through two gates at *[10. 15.13'/11.55', 3.85km/260m, 10 min]* and *[11. 14.98'/10.77', 5.06km/1.21km, 15 min].–* on the way you will have views across to the metochis of Christ of the Nuns and St Nikolaos Planas.

After the second gate the kalderimi continues along the edge of a terrace to meet the outbound track near its start just below the road *[12. 14.97'/10.74', 5.11km/50m, 3 min].* The kalderimi continues at the top of the bank opposite, and leads diagonally up to the road, where there is a crash barrier. It is easier and safer to turn left on the track and retrace your outward route back to Leimonos *[13. 14.88'/10.40', 5.82km/710m, 10 min].*

Parakoila: its Minaret and Coast

18

Total distance 4¾ kilometres

 Walking time 1½ hours

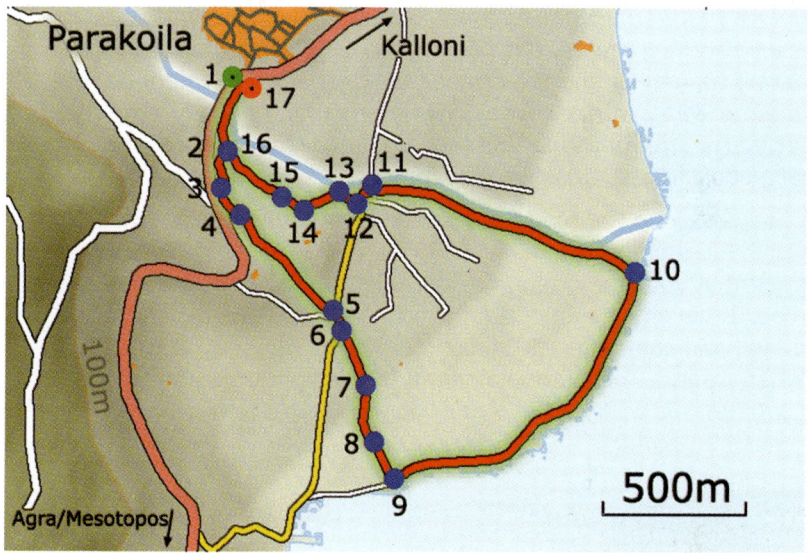

Parakoila (Παράκοιλα) is a prosperous village on the Gulf of Kalloni about 11 km south of Kalloni on the road to Agra and Mesopotos. Under Ottoman rule it was a joint Greek and Turkish settlement, and is now mainly of interest to outsiders for the remains of the mosque to the south-east of the village, with the one surviving complete minaret in Lesvos, though if you look back towards the lower edge of the village from the starting-point of the walk you will also see the almost intact remains of the old Turkish bathhouse, or hamam.

The village lies above the main road, on the right as you come from Kalloni. To reach the start of the walk drive along the main road, passing a filling station on the right, until you reach a lay-by with a bus-shelter. Park here, trying to leave room for the occasional bus which stops here on its way to Mesopotos.

If you want to explore the village before or after your walk go up the street just beyond the lay-by, and continue uphill. The village square, with cafenions and a few small shops, is near the top left of the village (as viewed from the main road). A street leads out of the top of the square and bends right to run north-east along the top of the village parallel with the main road below. About 250 metres along at a junction on the right is a shop belonging to the flourishing Women's Co-operative, selling their local products. There is a café a few metres downhill on the left (which may not be open during the day!), and the street continues down to the main road about 650m towards Kalloni from your parking place. In the maze of attractive streets within this box are the village school, a number of small businesses, and two churches.

Continue along the road for a few metres until you come to a stone water fountain on the right *[1. 39°10.03'/26°08.39']*. Follow the track that you see forking off to the left on the opposite side of the road. It becomes a kalderimi, which leads over an ancient stone bridge and continues with a concrete water channel on the left. When it forks, follow the kalderimi to the right on a narrower path *[2. 09.90'/08.35', 270m, 5 min]*.

The path leads back towards the road: a few metres before it reaches it, turn left across a stream bed *[3. 09.83'/08.33', 420m/150m, 5 min]* and go up to join another track. Turn left and follow it – there are traces of an old kalderimi path on the left-hand edge. It goes over a slight rise and down, before veering right at a field entrance *[4. 09.78'/08.39', 570m/150m, 3 min]*. The ruins of the old mosque, and its minaret, are close by in the field immediately to your left.

Continue on the track as it bears right uphill to go over a low ridge, with the chapel of Αγ Ιωάννης (St John) on a mound over to the left, and then runs downhill to meet an asphalt road *[5. 09.60'/08.62', 1.04km/470m, 10 min]*. (If you wish to visit the chapel, there is a path leading up to it on the return leg of your walk.)

Turn right on the road for a few metres until it bends slightly to the right, then take the narrow track off to the left *[6. 09.57'/08.63', 1.10km/60m, 1 min]*, and when it forks keep right *[7. 09.47'/08.70', 1.31km/210m, 5 min]*.

Walk along the track, with a fenced olive grove on your right, and when it turns sharp left at a gate follow it until it ends at the

entrances to two fields *[8. 09.37'/08.71', 1.51km/200m, 5 min]*.
Go into the right-hand field and head for a gap in the reed hedge
diagonally across from you. Go through the gap (there is a ditch
here which may contain water!) and continue across the next field
towards a ruined building. Leave the building to your right and come
out on to a sandy beach *[9. 09.30'/08.76', 1.66km/150m, 5 min]*.

**NB. These are cultivated fields: if there are any signs of
growing crops, including grass (which will be harvested for
hay or silage) please walk round the edge of the fields to
avoid trampling them.**

Turn left along the beach. A track emerges from the left and
briefly runs along to a house. Follow it, and when it ends, continue
on the beach until a path disappears inland through high reeds
[10. 09.68'/09.35', 2.92km/1.26km, 15 min]. (It is quite easy to
miss this path: if you reach a river-mouth you have gone about
200m too far!)

Turn left along the path. It passes a cottage on the right,
and becomes a track running alongside the river. When it
reaches an asphalt road at a bridge crossing the river, turn left
[11. 09.83'/08.71', 3.90km/980m, 15 min].

Follow the road for 50 metres and then take the first track to the
right *[12. 09.81'/08.67', 3.95km/50m, 2 min]*. It returns to the
river-bank (the chapel you passed earlier is now above you to
the left). In less than 100 metres a path goes left across a water-
channel and immediately right *[13. 09.83'/08.62', 4.03km/80m,
2 min]*.

Follow this narrow, walled path, and turn right at the next
junction on to a path running alongside the water-channel.
[14. 09.79'/08.54', 4.17km/140m, 3 min]. (To visit the chapel keep
ahead here and then bear left uphill.)

When the path divides keep left, with the channel now on your
right *[15. 09.81'/08.49', 4.25km/80m, 2 min]*. Keep left at the
next junction, and at the T-junction immediately ahead turn right
[16. 09.90'/08.35', 4.49km/240m, 6 min].

This was point 2 on your outward route. Walk back along the
kalderimi and over the old bridge to return to your starting point
[17. 10.03'/08.39', 4.76km/270m, 6 min].

Around Skala Eresou – the Village, its Kampos, and its Beach

19

Total distance 7¼ kilometres

 Walking time 2¼ hours

Like many other Lesvos towns which now lie several kilometres inland, the first known settlement of Eresos was on the coast, in an acropolis on the hill called Vigla (Βίγλα) on the southern edge of the modern Skala Eresou. It was inhabited since at least 600BC, and was the birthplace not only of the pre-eminent classical poet Sappho (Σαπφώ), known as 'the tenth muse', but also of the philosopher Theophrastos (Θεόφραστος), a friend, protégé and successor of Aristotle, who became known as the 'father of botany', and his

contemporary and colleague, the historian Phanias (Φαινίας).

In modern times the fertile kampos between Eresos and Skala Eresou became famous for its figs and mulberries, while Skala Eresou itself has developed into a laid-back holiday resort, benefitting from its two kilometres of soft sandy beach, and its association with Sappho, seen, rightly or wrongly, as the original gay feminist, which has brought an annual women's festival here each September.

This easy, mostly level walk shows you the main features of the ancient and modern town, takes you through the varied small-scale agriculture of the kampos, and finishes with the opportunity for a swim somewhere along the long beach, and a meal in one of the many beach-side tavernas.

Skala Eresou is about 50km from Kalloni, either via Vatoussa and Antissa to the north, or Agra and Mesopotos to the south. Both are good, if winding roads, through very different and equally spectacular scenery, and we recommend that you go by one route and return by the other. As you arrive at Skala Eresou there is a large car-park on the right of the road: park here.

While you are in the area, you might like to visit the 17th century Pithari Monastery (Μονή Πιθαρίου), near Eresos. It is beautifully situated above a recently created man-made lake in a deep valley. To reach it take the Mesopotos road from its junction on the Eresou – Skala Eresou road, and turn left after 900m immediately after crossing a river. This dirt road brings you to the dam at the foot of the lake: continue along the right-hand side of the lake to reach the monastery.

The walk starts at the corner of the car park by the cross roads *[1. 39°08.15′/25°55.87′]*. Turn left from the road you arrived on, and follow the street along, climbing gently, as far as the crossing at the village church of Άγιος Ανδρέας (St Andrew) *[2. 08.09′/55.95′, 170m, 3 min]*.

Turn left and walk along the street for a few metres. Behind the church are the remains of a 5th or 6th century AD basilica, and sections of its mosaic floor. In a courtyard on the opposite side of the street is the local archaeological museum. At the time of writing it is closed, and its contents have been removed to the museum in Mitilini, but there is a local campaign to have it re-opened.

Return to the crossing and go ahead until you reach the sea *[3. 08.05′/55.92′, 290m/120m, 7 min]*. Turn left and walk along the paved road past a continuous row of attractive beach bars, with shaded decks cantilevered out over the beach. When they end continue along under the cliffs, passing modern sculptures evoking the spirit of Sappho, until you come to a small fishing harbour *[4. 07.87′/56.14′, 785m/495m, 10 min]*.

The road ends here. A little further on there is a small chapel under the cliffs, but go to the left up a small path leading up away from the sea opposite the end of the harbour breakwater. As it rises you will see, on the upper slopes of Vigla, the hill to your left, two surviving towers from the 14th century AD Gatelouzo castle, the final fortifications on the site of the acropolis of Eresos. If you want a closer view there is a small path leading up the hillside.

The path bends right and left and leads to the end of a lane *[5. 07.93′/56.31′, 1.13km/345m, 12 min]*.

Go along the lane, and when it reaches a T-junction bear left, towards a large house on top of a hill ahead *[6. 08.06′/56.47′, 1.46km/330m, 7 min]*.

At the next junction go ahead on the lesser track *[7. 08.13'/56.47', 1.61km/150m, 5 min]*, and at the next, where a concrete track (which is also a stream-bed) goes off to the left, go straight ahead again *[8. 08.41'/56.49', 2.18km/570m, 8 min]*.

Continue on this track, ignoring side turnings to right and left, until you come to crossing track *[9. 08.67'/56.44', 2.69km/510m, 7 min]*. Go ahead again, and then bend left at a farm, when the track becomes concrete (and in wet weather a stream-bed). Go on until you come to a T-junction, and turn left on to a concrete road with a river on your right *[10. 08.79'/56.10', 3.40km/710m, 13 min]*.

This soon joins the road from Eresos to Skala Eresou *[11. 08.78'/55.94', 3.64km/240m, 3 min]*. Turn right over the bridge, and then immediately left along the asphalt road along the other side of the river.

Take the second track on the right *[12. 08.70'/55.77', 3.97km/330m, 8 min]*. It leads uphill between two houses and comes to a fork. Ignore the concrete track down to the left, and go

up over the brow of the rise towards the hills on the far side of the plain. When you come to a T-junction turn left *[13. 08.82'/55.49', 4.46km/490m, 7 min]*.

Go along the track, heading towards the sea. Ahead of you to the left you will see the buildings of a resort hotel, and on the right of the track low volcanic cliffs and giant rocks with large boulders and stones embedded in them. Beyond these cliffs, the track bends away to the right towards the hills that mark the end of the kampos and Skala Eresou beach. (A clear track up the hillside degenerates into a path that leads to the chapel of Profitis Ilias *(Προφήτης Ηλίας)*, high above the sea 1½km away).

Your track bends back to the left and comes to a T-junction with the dirt road running behind the sand-dunes that back the beach *[14. 08.39'/55.06', 5.65km/1.19km, 15 min]*.

Go straight across, and cross the dunes on to the beach. A few metres along the beach to your right there is a seasonal refreshment shack, and on the hillside beyond a white-painted female symbol (♀), a reminder of the annual Women's Festival.

Turn left along the beach. The resort hotel hosts activity holidays, and during the season there are almost always sailing, sail-boarding, and other water-sports going on along this stretch. Walk along the soft sand until you come to the river mouth *[15. 08.19'/55.53', 6.55km/900m, 15 min]*.

You should be able to cross the river with ease, but if you are doubtful return to the nearest beach bar, go down to its left, turn right on to the road and follow it over a bridge. Turn right on the far side of the bridge, and go through the adjacent car-park back to the beach.

Then continue along the beach until you come to the beginning of the paved walk and the first tavernas *[16. 08.12'/55.75', 6.92km/370m, 6 min]*. Walk along until you come to the small central square, dominated by a modern statue of Sappho, and a bust of Theophrastos *[17. 08.08'/55.86', 7.07km/150m, 3 min]*.

Now turn left out of the square, and walk away from the sea along the main street, which leads back to the car-park *[18. 08.15'/55.87', 7.20km/130m, 3 min]*.

Olives, Cliffs, Rocks and Sea:-
Liota and Ligeri to Gavathas

20

Total distance 5¼ kilometres

 Walking time 2 hours

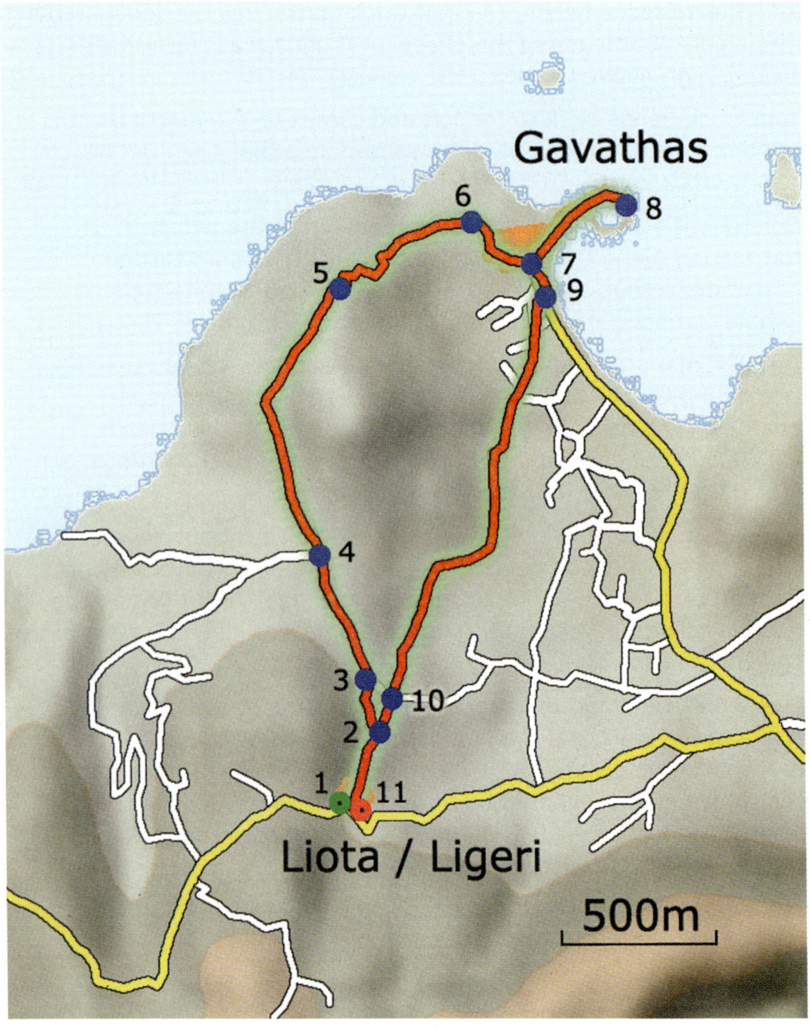

Gavathas

Liota / Ligeri

500m

Some maps call the village on the hillside above the fishing harbour of Gavathas (Γαββαθάς) on the north-west coast of Lesvos Ligeri (Λυγερή), some Liota (Λιώτα), never both. In fact it is both, two tiny settlements joined by a concrete street and so close together that you cannot see the join. Approaching by car, the road signs point you to Liota, and that is where the asphalt road ends, at a paved square under a plane tree, next to a taverna with a terrace looking down to the sea, and little else.

According to legend, the names come from the Byzantine princess Ligeri, who was isolated in a tower here suffering from leprosy. In her solitude, she was constantly roaming about the countryside, and became known as 'λιώστρα πριγκίπισσα' – 'the wandering princess', hence 'Λιώτα'. One day she saw a leprous pig roll in the mud and emerge cured. She followed its example and was cured likewise. In thanksgiving her father the emperor built the church of 'Παναγία Λιώτας', Our Lady of Liota.

This easy walk starts here, and takes you through olive groves and around the coast high above the sea, with beautiful views across to the inaccessible north-west corner of the island, before descending to the little fishing harbour of Gavathas. There have been various failed attempts over the years to establish Gavathas as a holiday

resort, but if you can ignore the shell of a large unfinished apartment block, it remains unspoilt, and with one taverna and a long sandy beach is an attractive place to spend an hour or two before going on.

To reach Liota take the road from Kalloni to Sigri and Eresos through Vatoussa (Βατούσσα), and after 7 kilometres (2km before Antissa) turn right towards Gavathas. Follow this road for 4 kilometres, turn left at the junction signposted Liota (Λιώτα), and go on for 1½ kilometres until the road ends..

Start in the square *[1. 39°16.04'/25°57.95']*, and go in front of the taverna on to the concrete road out towards the sea. At the first junction, immediately before a modern house, turn left up the concrete road *[2. 16.16'/58.00', 263m, 5 min]*. Follow it up and round to the right over the brow of the hill. Ignore a track off to the right and descend to a T-junction *[3. 16.25'/57.97', 460m/197m, 5 min]*.

Turn left, and follow the track through olive groves. At the next junction ignore the track off to the left *[4. 16.45'/57.87', 830m/370m, 7 min]*, (this leads to the bay and beach that you will soon see down to your left), but continue straight ahead.

The track climbs, following the coastline, with spectacular views towards Lapsarna and Cape Fournia. It leads uphill to end at farm buildings on a bluff overlooking Gavathas *[5. 16.90'/57.94', 1.80km/970m, 22 min]*.

A path leads to the left below the bluff, turns sharp right, and then winds downhill. (The lower part of the path is clearly visible from the bluff – the beginning is fairly inconspicuous. If you have difficulty finding it, go down to the trees further over to the right, then left to join the path further down). The path leads through a gate and gets steeper with loose stones. In wet weather it becomes a stream; take it with care, and be prepared to go through the thorn bushes alongside if necessary. It leads down, across a field, and ends at a fence. There is no gate, but a block of concrete and a lowered fence provide a stile *[6. 17.00'/58.21', 2.37km/570m, 20 min]*.

Cross the fence, and turn right on to the lane beyond. Bear right down the concrete street to the junction at the bottom of the hill *[7. 16.94'/58.34', 2.60km/230m, 9 min].* Here turn right, and immediately left, and walk along the shore to the picturesque fishing harbour, protected by striking russet volcanic rocks *[8. 17.04'/58.56', 3.01km/410m, 7 min].*

Return from the harbour along the shore road, and follow it round to the solitary beach taverna *[9. 16.89'/58.38', 3.54km/530m, 10 min]*. Turn right up the side of the taverna, and at the end of the street turn left at the T-junction.

Follow the concrete lane out of the village. After the last house it becomes a dirt track, but reverts to concrete on-and-off for the rest of the route. The track passes a group of ruined cottages and starts to climb, and after a final steep climb on concrete reaches Ligeri. At the junction here continue ahead bearing slightly left *[10. 16.20'/58.03', 4.99km/1.45km, 25 min]*.

A few metres further on at the next junction you rejoin your outbound route: continue ahead to return to the welcoming taverna at Liota *[11. 16.04'/57.95', 5.32km/330m, 6 min]*.

Kampos Beach and Ancient Antissa

21

Total distance 11 kilometres

 Walking time 2¾ hours

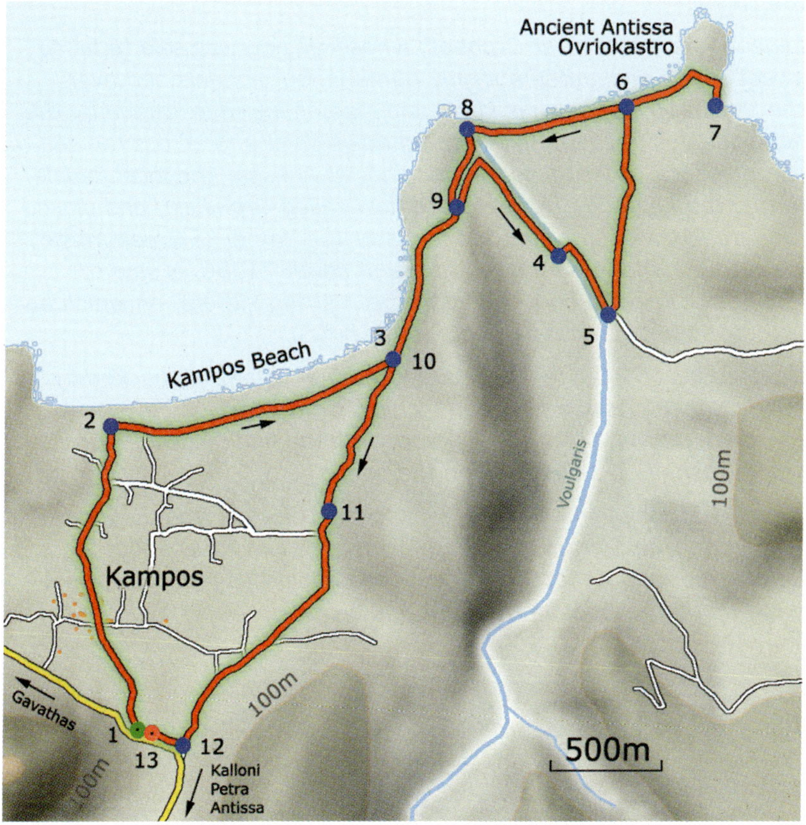

Ancient Antissa (Αρχαία Άντισσα) was first settled in the tenth century BC, and became one of the six founding city states of Lesvos. It is believed that the site was then an off-shore island, which later became joined to the mainland as the result of an earthquake. The city came under Athenian dominance after the

Peloponnesian war of 428BC, having been on the wrong side, with Mitilini, in revolt against the Athenian League. It survived until 168BC, when it was completely destroyed by the Romans and the surviving inhabitants removed to Mithimna in retribution for their support of Perseus of Macedonia against Rome. The ruins visible today are those of the Ovriokastro (Οβριόκαστρο – 'Castle of the Hebrew'), one of the series of castles built or extended by the medieval Genoese Gatelouzi rulers before the Ottoman conquest of the island.

Legend has it that after Orpheus, whose singing was said to be so sweet that it enchanted not only humans, but animals and even the trees and stones, was killed and dismembered in Thrace by the Maenads, his head and lyre floated down-river and across the sea to come ashore, still singing and playing, at Antissa. The local people buried the head nearby at a place now called Orphikeia, and placed the lyre in their temple of Apollo. Later the 'father of Greek music', Terpander, who was born in Antissa in about 710BC, is said to have been inspired by it to invent the 7-string kithera, on which he composed the accompaniments to his lyrics.

Kampos beach is an idyllic 1½km stretch of soft sand, backed by dunes, ideal for swimming and picnics. On the sea-bed off-shore there are petrified tree-trunks, and you may find pieces of petrified wood washed up as pebbles on the beach.

To reach the beginning of the walk follow the road from Kalloni to Eressos and Sigri, and turn right towards Gavathas about 2km before 'modern' Antissa. Go about 3km down this road, passing a large modern chapel on the right and a cement works away to the

left. Shortly afterwards at a left-hand bend there is a track to the right signposted to ΚΑΜΠΟΣ. This will be on your return route: for now continue 300m further down the road, cross a bridge (also with a sign 'Προς ΠΑΡΑΛΙΑ ΚΑΜΠΟΣ To The BEACH KAMPOS), and park a little further on, by a gate on the left-hand side of the road, being careful to leave the entrance clear.

Standing on the bridge, look downstream to the concrete surfaced and walled lane below. This is one of the many lanes on Lesvos and other Greek islands that in the rainy season will become a river, but during spring and summer the banks above the walls are rich with oregano, lavender, capers, and pomegranates *[1. 39°15.91'/25°59.39']*. Go down the ramp and along the lane until you reach the beach *[2. 16.63'/59.30', 1.40km, 20 min]*. (Do not forget to obey the rather incongruous STOP sign at a crossing near the halfway point!).

Turn right along the sandy track behind the beach, with views back through the dunes to Gavathas, or if you prefer walk along the soft sand of the beach itself. The track eventually joins a wider one coming in from the right at a picnic pavilion *[3. 39°16.79'/26°00.18', 2.75km/1.35km, 15 min]*.

Keep left, heading towards a cape, and walk along under red cliffs. The track rises to cross behind the cape: at the brow ancient Antissa comes into sight across a fertile river valley on the next promontory, with the rival (and more successful) ancient city of Molivos behind it in the far distance. The track leads back down towards the sea: ignore a track off to the right and continue on the main track, following it round to the right as it begins to run inland alongside the river Voulgaris (Βούλγαρης).

Go on alongside the river until you reach a crossing point shortly before a cottage on the right of the track (there will probably be several pieces of earth-moving machinery, in various states of disrepair, parked alongside the track here) *[4. 17.02'/00.68', 4.31km/1.56km, 30 min]*.

Cross the river (if there is too much water here, there is an alternative crossing about 350m further upstream) and turn right along the track on the opposite bank. When you come to a T-junction turn left (the alternative crossing point is here), and immediately left again leaving a modern water-fountain on your left

[5. 16.89'/00.82', 4.76km/450m, 10 min].

Follow this track as it winds through fields back to the sea and turns right along the shingle beach *[6. 17.33'/00.88', 5.64km/880m, 10 min].* Continue on the track behind the beach, past a seasonal beach taverna, towards the remains of the ancient kastro on the headland, and when you reach it follow the track round to the right under its walls.

There is a narrow entrance to the kastro near this corner, with a footpath leading up to it. However the interior is not maintained, holds little of interest, and is a popular home for snakes, so we recommend that you do not visit. If you do, please make sure you are wearing boots and heavy trousers, and take great care.

The track leads on into the next bay, where there are the remains of the harbour of the ancient city, and a modern picnic pavilion where you can take a half-way break in the shade *[7. 17.36'/01.16', 6.22km/580m, 10 min].* We turn back at this point, but if you wish to explore further there is a chapel and a few other buildings further on along the shore (the taverna that used to be here is, sadly, no more).

Walk back past the kastro and along the beach until you reach the river-mouth *[8. 17.31'/00.39', 7.50km/1.28km, 22 min].* Cross the river on the shingle bank and turn left inland. Follow the river-bank for a few metres then bear right uphill to meet the end of a field track. Follow this uphill (parallel with the track that you came down on the outward leg of the walk) towards the top of the field, then bear left to a gate *[9. 17.11'/00.36', 7.96km/460m, 10 min].*

Go through the gate, turn right on to the track, and retrace your steps as far as the junction with the Kampos beach track *[10. 16.79'/00.18', 8.64km/680m, 10 min].*

Keep straight ahead on the main left-hand track. (If you prefer, and would like to end your walk with a swim, you can of course return along the beach from here and follow the outward route back to the start.) Pass a derelict tank on your right, which has been parked here for many years, with its gun kept in working order, as a defence against possible invasion!

Walk along along the track away from the sea, passing a large modern chapel down on the right, with an immaculate paved and walled entrance (the tiny original chapel nestles inconspicuously next to the track). At the next junction bear left uphill *[11. 39°16.45'/25°59.97', 9.37km/730m, 10 min],* and continue, ignoring further turnings to the right, until you reach an asphalt road *[12. 15.86'/59.53', 10.70km/1.33km, 17 min].* Turn right on to the road, and walk downhill back to your starting point at the bridge *[13. 15.91'/59.39', 11.00km/300m, 5 min].*

A Forest Walk around Vatoussa and Pterounta

22

Total distance 10 kilometres

Walking time 3 hours

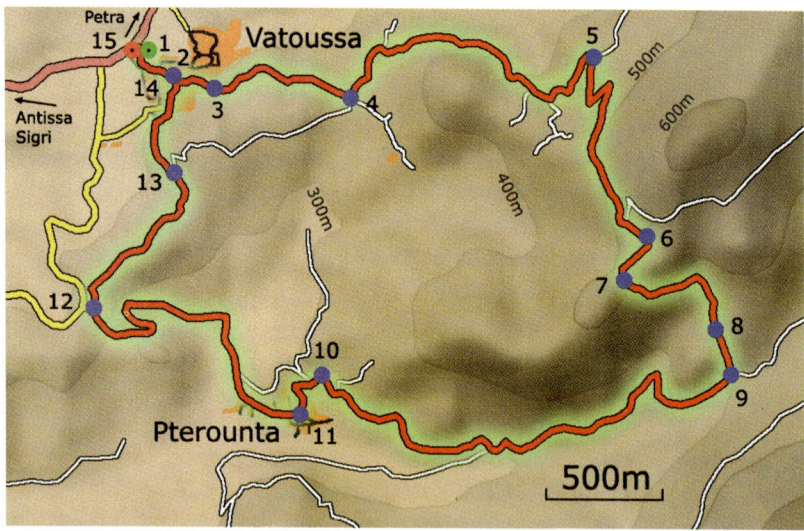

This walk takes you through the western edge of the pine forest that covers the high volcanic hills between the Gulf of Kalloni and the much starker landscape towards the west of the island. It starts in the traditional village of Vatoussa (Βατούσσα), whose beautiful, well kept houses and mansions, paved streets, and unchanging cafenions and businesses befit its protected status, and make it well worth exploring before or after your walk.

From Vatoussa you climb through the forest, to an altitude of 500 metres, with beautiful views across the island, before descending along a tiny footpath to a forest road which leads past thickets of Rhododendron luteum, which in Greece grows wild only in this part of Lesvos, and strikingly coloured volcanic rock formations, to bring you to the sleepy village of Pterounta (Πτερούντα), and finally along a hillside track back to Vatoussa.

While you are in this area, you might also like to visit the nearby village of Chidera (Χίδηρα). This is the home of the local organic Methimneos wine, made from locally-grown traditional grape varieties. It was also the birthplace of the artist Georgios Iakovidis (1853-1932), designer of the Statue of Liberty in Mitilini, and first director of the Greek Nation Art Gallery. His work is on display in the first digital art gallery in Greece, established here in his memory.

Vatoussa is about 25km from Kalloni on the road to Antissa, Eresos and Sigri. The entrance to the village is on a sharp bend where there are two cafenions, a water-fountain, and a tiny tree-shaded park. There is a car-park a few metres on the left towards Antissa.

The walk starts at the water-fountain, where a paved street leads up into the village *[1. 39°13.59'/026°02.96']*. Walk up the street, and at the first junction bear left (sign-posted 'Post'). Stay on this street as it bends right and left until you come to a T-junction at a marble water-fountain with the dedication ΓΡΗΓΟΡΙΟΣ ΓΩΓΟΣ ΑΡΧΙΜΑΝΔΡΙΤΗΣ 1899 (Grigorios Gogos Archimandritis – the 19th century Gogos mansion elsewhere in the village is now a museum).

Above it is the church of the Dormition of the Virgin, one of the two large churches in the village *[2. 13.53'/03.07', 195m, 5 min]*.

Turn right and almost immediately come into the village centre: there are shops and cafenions, with the church, built in 1850, and the community offices (KOINOTIKON KATAΣTHMA BATOYΣHΣ) in a small square on your left. Go left up steps (OΔOΣ TZEÏMΣΠAPIΣ), past a tiny traditional bakery, whose bread, baked in a wood-fired oven, is sold through its open window, and at the top cross and continue ahead, keeping the tall house on the junction to your right.

Take the next right turn, then, at a house with red pointing, right again, and follow the street to the edge of the village, where the paving ends and it becomes a path *[3. 13.50'/03.19', 450m/255m, 10 min]*.

Follow this path: it leads round to the left through meadows along the side of a valley, then crosses a rocky section, bears right and continues to meet a crossing track *[4. 13.48'/03.60', 1.07km/620m, 17 min]*.

Turn left on to the track and follow it as it climbs into woodland,

first mainly oaks, then, higher up, into pine forest. Stay on it when it swings sharp right uphill, ignoring the traces of a disused track leading ahead downhill *[5. 13.57'/04.32', 2.39km/1.32km, 30 min].*

It zig-zags up through the forest, then emerges, more than 500 metres above sea level, to run along the edge of a valley with open views across to the west towards the village of Chidera, the wind-farm on the far ridge beyond Antissa, and the sea far below in the distance to your right.

Continue to a T-junction *[6. 13.17'/04.48', 3.44km/1.05km, 20 min],* and turn right on to a broad track, which leads on downhill for a little more than 200 metres before coming to an end *[7. 13.08'/04.40', 3.66km/220m, 5 min].*
There is a small path leading ahead into the forest from the end of the track. Follow it downhill and round the end of a valley. It crosses a stream and rises, before apparently ending on the edge of an open area with the ruins of a stone animal shelter in front of a rocky outcrop over to the right *[8. 12.97'/04.68', 4.24km/580m, 20 min].*

This is a good spot for a break: when you are ready to continue go on along the line of the path down the left-hand side of the valley that drops away through the forest from the shelter. There are traces of a path, but you will soon see a forest road ahead of you through the trees. As you approach bear to the right into the bottom of the valley to make it easier to join the road. *[9. 12.88'/04.72', 4.44km/200m, 12 min].*

Turn right on to the forest road and follow it, with a river in the valley on your left, until you see the village of Pterounta below you on the left. On the way you will pass strikingly coloured volcanic rock formations in the cliffs alongside the road, and in spring the flowering golden rhododendrons.

At the junction above the outskirts of the village *[10. 12.86'/03.51', 6.72km/2.28km, 30 min]* bear left and follow the concrete street down to the first cross-roads *[11. 12.77'/03.44', 6.99km/270m, 3 min].*

Turn right, and follow the paved street through the village. Pass the cafenion and the large village church on your left, and then, when the stone paving gives way to asphalt at the further edge of the village, carry on along the road past a playground on the right, and continue as it winds uphill. When you reach the brow of the hill, immediately before a T-junction, turn right up a track *[12. 13.00'/02.82', 8.52km/1.53km, 22 min]*.

Follow this as it undulates round the hillside, and at the first fork take the lesser track downhill to the left *[13. 13.31'/03.07', 9.30km/780m, 15 min]*. It soon joins the end of a paved street: carry on down this street, keeping straight ahead at all junctions, until you come back to the village centre. From here retrace your route from the beginning of the walk, turning left at the water-fountain *[14. 13.53'/03.07', 9.77km/470m, 10 min]*, and then right, left, and right again to return to your starting point *[15. 13.59'/02.96', 9.97km/195m, 5 min]*.

Anemotia, Monastirelli and Golden Rhododendrons

23

Total distance 7½ kilometres

 Walking time 2½ hours

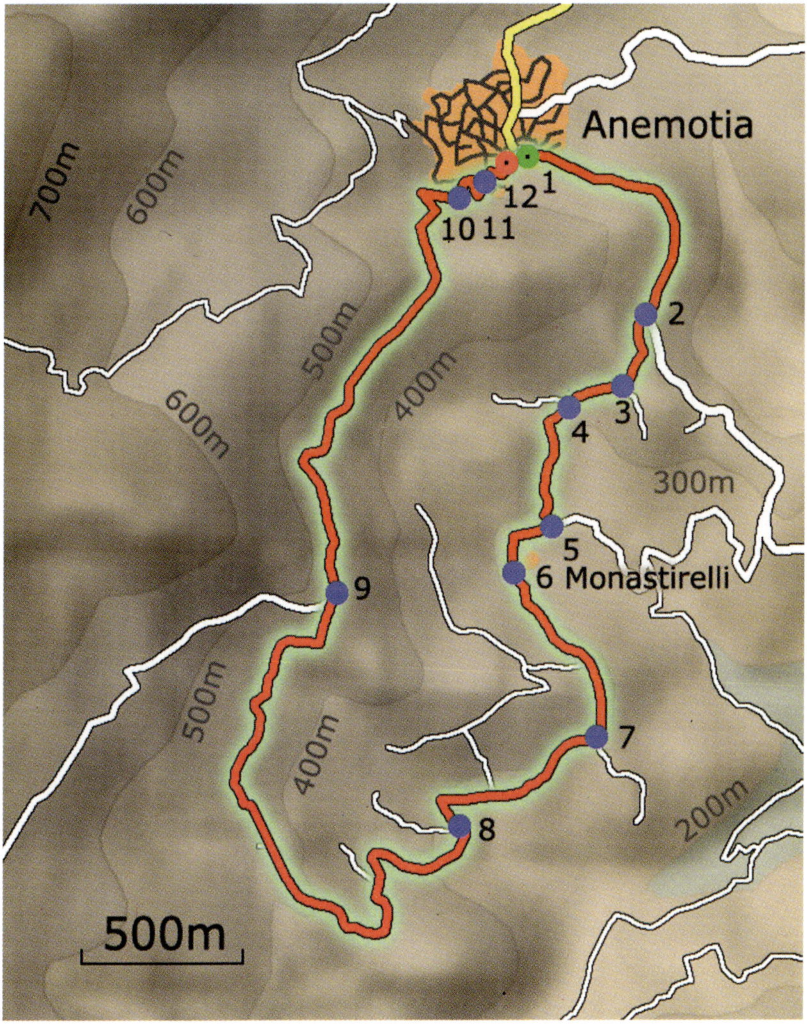

Anemotia

12 1
10 11

2

4 3

300m

5
6 Monastirelli

9

7

8

500m

200m

The mountain village of Anemotia (Ανεμότια) is situated north-west of Kalloni, 'στου ανεμού τα ότα', literally 'in the ears of the wind'. Lying 400 metres above sea level at the head of an east-facing valley, part of the crater of one of the largest (extinct) volcanoes on Lesvos, the wind is always strong here, and the snow stays longer on the roofs. In earlier times, many villagers earned their living as stonemasons, and the many beautiful traditional stone houses still bear witness to their skills. Now it is a mainly agricultural village of about 700 inhabitants.

This walk begins and ends at the impressive village church of 'the Resurrection of Christ', and leads via a beautiful kalderimi to the 18th century monastery of the 'Entrance of the Theotokos' (Virgin Mary), otherwise known as Monastirelli. It is a dependency (μετόχη) of the monastery of Leimonos, and its former name of Voukolon suggests that it was used by monks from Leimonos working as shepherds (ο βουκόλος – shepherd).

The walk continues through forest, where in spring you will see the golden flowers of Rhododendron luteum, the only area in Greece where it grows in the wild, thanks to the unique acid soil resulting from the lava of volcanic eruptions fifteen to twenty million years ago, and finally returns to Anemotia along a high dirt road from which you can look down over your outward route to the Gulf of Kalloni.

Anemotia lies one kilometre to the south of the road from Kalloni to Skalachori and the west of the island, about 2.5km beyond the village of Filia. The turning off the main road is near the brow of a hill, and should be treated with care. Drive through the narrow

village street, past the cafenions and small shops, until you reach the church. There are a few parking spaces here – if none are free continue down the road to the grassy, tree-shaded island just before the local olive press, where you are sure to find room.

(Above the road before you enter the village you will see some of the panels of one of Lesvos's two major solar generation installations - the other is a few kilometres away at Skalachori. Built since 2010, each is designed to produce over 69,000kW.)

From the starting point at the church *[1. 39°14.71'/26°06.28']*, walk to the left along the road leading out of the village. You pass a children's playground above the road on your left, and then, after the road divides around a central island, under the overhead conveyor of the local olive press. (The presses and other machinery can be seen through the windows of the main building on the left.)

Go on along the road. It climbs gently along the hillside, with a deep valley on the left, part of the long-extinct volcanic crater, running down towards the Gulf of Kalloni. The road then bends around the hill and starts to descend. When it bends left take the small track leading ahead on the right *[2. 14.48'/06.58', 785m, 10 min]*.

Follow the track uphill until it ends at a small grassy level space, then take the footpath down to the right *[3. 14.34'/06.54', 1.07km/285m, 5 min].* It winds downhill, at first over a rocky outcrop, but soon becomes a narrow kalderimi for most of the rest of the way to the foot of the valley. Half-way down it forks: ignore the more obvious right-hand path (which simply leads into a field), and also a stream-bed to the left, and continue straight down *[4. 14.31'/06.42', 1.29km/220m, 10 min].*

When it reaches the bottom of the valley the path crosses above a stream, turns sharp left, and leads uphill to a gate. Go through the gate on to the end of a rough track, and follow it downhill to a T-junction *[5. 14.12'/06.38', 1.70km/410m, 14 min].*

Turn right here. Monastirelli immediately comes into view below on the left: follow the track down and round to its entrance *[6. 14.05'/06.30', 1.94km/240m, 5 min].* The monastery is not usually open to visitors, but through the gate there is a good view of its courtyard, dominated by a tall cypress tree, and the galleried monastic cells on either side. It is situated in an idyllic location, at the head of a deep wooded valley with views far down to the Gulf of Kalloni near Parakoila, and beyond. There is a picnic pavilion at a viewpoint a short distance further on to the left of the track if you want to rest and share the view for a while.

From the monastery, continue uphill on the track. Ignore a concrete track leading uphill to the right, and go on with more views down to the gulf on the left. Then bend right and keep right on the main track *[7. 13.78'/06.47', 2.58km/640m, 15 min].*

Descend through olive groves along the side of a valley, with pine forest ahead. Go across a concrete bridge, and briefly uphill, ignoring a further track back up to the right. Cross a second concrete bridge at the end of the valley, go sharp left and back uphill on the other side. At the top of the hill ignore the track going to the right into an olive grove *[8. 13.64'/06.18', 3.25km/670m, 15 min].* Instead continue ahead, bearing right almost immediately, and follow a hardly used track along the edge of a deep, narrow valley, with mixed woodland and rhododendrons on the other side.

The track finally bends round to the left on to a very short stretch of concrete, and climbs steeply along the edge of the valley through rhododendrons and arbutus (strawberry trees). It bends right and continues a long climb before at last bearing right again and descending briefly to level out across the end of a valley. Then there is a final climb to join the dirt road leading back to Anemotia [9. 14.02'/05.91', 5.35km/2.10km, 40 min].

Turn right on to the road and follow it downhill. You are now higher up at the end of the same valley as Monastirelli, and after about a kilometre you will see it far below to the right, easily recognisable by its cypress tree.

The dirt road finally leads steeply downhill, with a pine wood on the right, and becomes concrete. It makes a sharp right-hand bend and winds down through the pines, passing Anemotia's cemetery on the right, to come to a T-junction [10. 14.66'/06.17', 7.02km/1.67km, 30 min].

Turn right, and follow the road down round the other side of the cemetery and through a left-hand hairpin bend to the next junction [11. 14.67'/06.23', 7.20km/180m, 3 min].

Turn right again, and immediately left on to a paved street. Follow it downhill past the church to the junction, and the end of your walk [12. 14.34'/06.54', 7.34km/140m, 5 min].

A Nature Walk around the Waterfall of Klapados

24

Total distance 9½ kilometres

 Walking time 2¾ hours

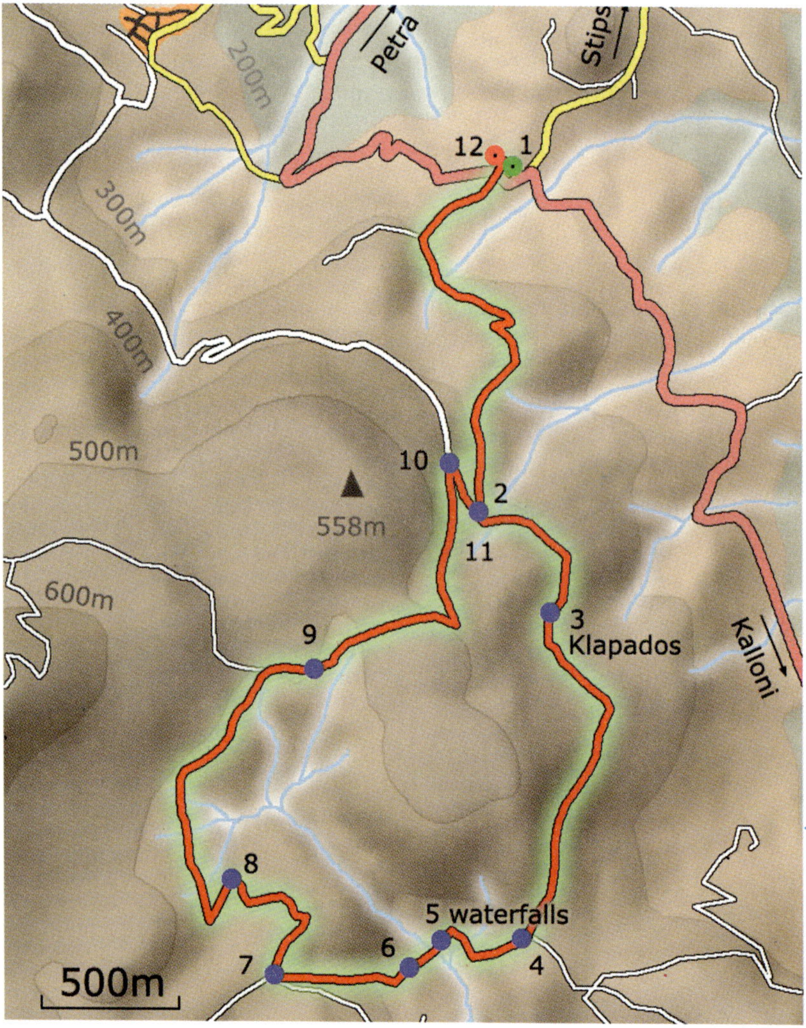

This walk takes you to the ruined village of Klapados, which is famous as the site of the final battle in the liberation of Lesvos, where the Ottoman garrison of Mitilini made its last stand before surrendering to Greek forces on 8 December 1912, thus liberating the island from 450 years of foreign rule. Hidden in a nearby valley, and much less well-known, is a seasonal waterfall, which falls about fifteen metres down a sheer cliff into a sheltered rock pool, rich in wild-life. From here the walk climbs further into the forest, through a rocky landscape full of ponds and wild flowers, to a final altitude of 500 metres, before returning to the starting point.

The walk starts on the main road from Kalloni to Petra about 5km south of Petra, where the road crosses the ridge at the end of the Lepetimnos mountain range west of Stipsi. Park off the road next to the hilltop taverna 'Ο ΓΑΒΡΙΛΟΣ'.

Start from the taverna *[1. 39°17.89'/26°11.61'],* cross the road and walk up the steep concrete track opposite. It soon loses the concrete surface as it winds uphill through olive groves, with views down to the coast at Petra to the right, and then to the Gulf of Kalloni on the left. It climbs into pine forest, and comes to a T-junction *[2. 17.24'/11.57', 1.64km, 25 min].*

Bear left, and follow the track until you reach the ruins of the old Ottoman village of Klapados *[3. 17.08'/11.75', 2.17km/530m, 10 min]*. The only identifiable building surviving from the old village is the domed-roof hamam, or bath-house, although until 1912 it was home to about eighty families, including a few Greeks, and the final three Greek families only left in 1960. Opposite the hamam a new, privately-built chapel, with a memorial to the Greek casualties of the brief military campaign that ended here, has been completed in time for the centenary of the liberation.

Continue along the track, with views across the olive groves of Lesvos's central valley, until you pass a large concrete water-reservoir on the right, and then come to a wide open area (there may be picnic tables here) *[4. 16.46'/11.71', 3.53km/1.36km, 15 min]*. Keep on the right-hand side of the field and go across to the rear corner, where a footpath leads away into the forest.

Follow this path downhill, bending right – it can be covered in pine-needles and difficult to follow in places. It ends at the pool at the foot of Klapados waterfall, under a massive old plane tree *[5. 16.46'/11.49', 3.88km/350m, 15 min]*. Even in summer, when the falls are dry, this is still a beautiful, shady and tranquil place for

a break: the pool is home to terrapins, frogs, and several varieties of dragon-fly, and it can be difficult to drag yourself away.

To continue, go downstream for a few metres, and cross the stream by the next tree. Follow a small path diagonally to the left up the opposite bank, and under a single-strand barbed-wire fence. Continue diagonally left up into a field, then bear right and walk across parallel with a stream down to your left. When you see a concrete barn on a low bluff on the left, cross the stream below it *[6. 16.41′/11.44′, 4.02km/140m, 10 min]*.

Work your way up to the barn, and go away from the valley along its long right-hand side (expect to find a pile of rotting timber partly blocking the way). Then immediately bear right on to a disused track leading uphill, and follow it along the side of the valley until

you see a parallel track above you on the left. Go up to join it and turn right *[7. 16.37'/11.11', 4.57km/550m, 15 min].*

A few metres further on you come to a gate at a T-junction. Turn right and continue on this wider track (there is often a small herd of contented and good-looking cattle grazing in the field on the right). The track climbs, bending left and then right. Along this stretch there are several ponds with terrapins, frogs, and dragonflies, and in spring and early summer you will see orchids and wild tulips.

The track descends, crosses a stream, and goes through a gate *[8. 16.54'/10.97', 5.20km/630m, 10 min].* Continue ahead, ignoring tempting tracks leading into the forest on the left. You climb along the edge of a valley, heading towards a high rocky ridge. The track bears right around the end of the ridge and comes to an open area on the right, with sharp rocky outcrops *[9. 16.97'/11.19', 6.63km/1.43km, 20 min].*

Here, at almost the highest point of the walk (about 500m), hidden in a large rock directly to your right, you will find the remains of an ancient shelter and stone animal shed once used by pastoral shepherds who lived here alongside their flocks.

Go on along the track: after a short distance it begins to descend, and from here on it is downhill all the way to the end of the walk. When you reach a T-junction turn right *[10. 17.33'/11.49', 7.69km/1.06km, 15 min],* go downhill for a short distance, and at the next junction turn left *[11. 17.24'/11.57', 7.89km/200m, 5 min].*

This was point 2 on the outward route. Now follow the track downhill to the road and the end of the walk (Take care on this final stretch – after rain the track can be deep in very slippery mud!) *[12. 17.89'/11.61', 9.53km/1.64m, 25 min].*

A Circular Walk from Skala Sikaminias

25

Total distance 7¾ kilometres

 Walking time 2½ hours

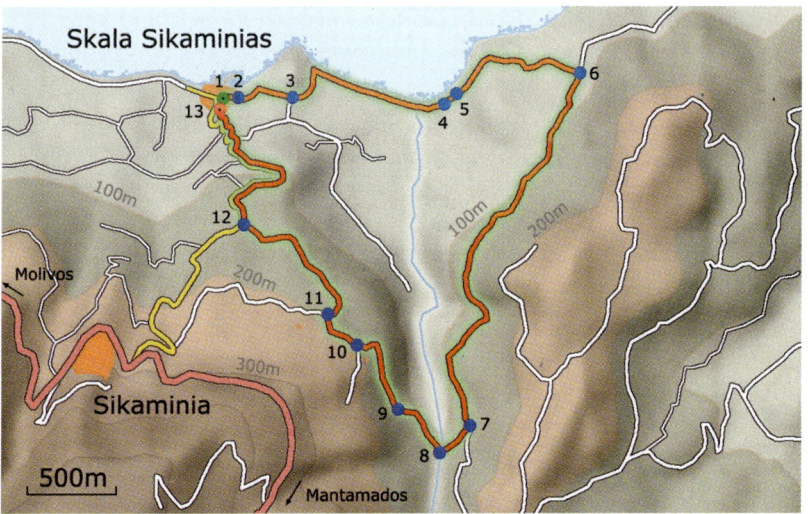

The beautiful fishing village of Skala Sikaminias was made famous by the local author Stratis Mirivillis with his novel 'The Mermaid Madonna', published in the 1950s, which was the origin of the apocryphal story of the wall painting of the Virgin Mary with the tail of a mermaid that was said to be displayed in the harbour church of Our Lady of the Fishermen (Παναγία των Ψαράδων). Today it is equally popular with visitors and local residents who are attracted as much by the harbourside tavernas as by the village's charm.

This walk starts from the harbour (if you can tear yourself and your companions away), takes you along a kalderimi over a headland to the neighbouring beach of Kagia (the best place for a swim) and then on tracks and little-used paths on a circuit along the coast and through the river valley behind, on the way visiting a hidden waterfall and spring. You should be back in Skala Sikaminias in time for a late lunch: everyone has their own favourite taverna here – we leave you to find yours.

Note that this walk can be difficult in places: there is river crossing which although short, can be treacherous when the water is high. There are also stretches of narrow path which can be very overgrown with brambles at any time of year. You will need strong, preferably water-resistant, shoes with non-slip soles, and trousers in heavy denim or other thorn-proof material. Shorts are definitely not suitable. A stick is also recommended both for pushing your way through brambles, and for disturbing any snakes which may be hidden in the undergrowth.

Skala Sikaminias is at the bottom of a long hill from its 'parent' mountain village of Sikaminia, which is on the road from Mantamados to Molyvos that runs along the north face of the Lepetymnos range. Sikaminia is 10 kilometres from Mantamados and 17½ from Molivos; the turning to the Skala is on the Mantamados edge of the village.

The walk starts facing the harbour of Skala Sikaminias, in front of the tavernas that line the quay *[1. 39°22.42'/26°18.19']*. Go to the right around the quayside, and then along the narrow stony beach.

At the far end a kalderimi runs uphill along the cliff-edge *[2. 22.42'/18.30', 155m, 5 min]*.

Follow the kalderimi as it climbs over the headland. Looking back you will have panoramic views of Skala Sikaminias – somewhere along here was the viewpoint used by the Lesviot primitive artist Theophilos for his painting of the village in 1933. It eventually bends to the right and becomes a concrete track running downhill. (Should the steel gates on the left at this point be open, do not be tempted by the track leading uphill back towards the cliff). Carry on down for a few metres until the track meets a tarmac road, then turn left *[3. 22.41'/18.46', 410m/255m, 7 min]*.

Follow the road down to Kagia beach, then turn right along the dirt road behind the beach. When the road peters out continue along the beach (depending on the time of year you may encounter two streams crossing your path). There is a high old stone wall, possibly built as a protection against pirates, separating the beach from the land behind, and beyond that a small headland with a path over the rocks. Go on to the end of the beach *[4. 22.40'/19.07', 1.43km/1.02km, 15 min]*, and then go to the right for a couple of metres to find the beginning of a small path leading uphill to the left.

The path winds up along the top of the cliffs until it joins the end of an overgrown track *[5. 22.42'/19.11', 1.50km/70m, 5 min]*. Continue on the track, crossing a cattle-grid (there may be a brushwood barrier here). At a crossing track go straight on, through a gate. The track bends right away from the coast: there are old olive trees on the left, and a belt of pines on the right. Go over a second cattle grid, and then uphill to a third, immediately before a T-junction *[6. 22.49'/19.58', 2.30km/800m, 15 min]*.

Turn right and follow the wide track along the side of a wide valley, with views back to Kagia on the right. The track climbs, then descends, and the hill village of Sikaminia comes into view across the valley to the right, backed by the twin peaks of Vigla (with Olympos in the south, the joint highest mountain on the island) and Mirivilli. Shortly afterwards you will see the village of Kleio on the hill ahead, after which the track swings to the left, and then back to the right.

When you see a tempting path leading off into olive groves on the right at a left-hand bend, ignore it, but watch out for the farm buildings which are on the right a short distance further on. Immediately after them, and a slight right-hand bend, look for a path into a field on the right (there may be several steel-

mesh animal pens on the right of the field) *[7. 21.47'/19.16', 4.74km/2.44km, 30 min].*

Go down the path with the pens on your right; it gradually gets steeper and finally becomes a stream bed (if there is too much water for comfort go into the field on the right and walk down alongside the wall, rejoining the path at the bottom of the hill) before reaching a river *[8. 21.39'/19.08', 4.86km/120m, 7 min].*

Cross the river. Take great care: there are stepping stones but they are very slippery when wet – if in doubt find an alternative crossing. Then follow the kalderimi opposite, which zig-zags uphill – the path is clear but if in doubt at any point keep to the right. It becomes a level, overgrown path along the side of the valley, with a terrace wall on the left. It finally bends to the left and reaches an old stone cistern *[9. 21.50'/18.19', 5.12km/260m, 15 min].*

From the cistern continue ahead, through a group of five poplar trees, up a bank to a terrace wall. Turn right (not left on to the clearer path!) up a path to the foot of a small waterfall. Go across to the right and up a stream bed for a few metres, then cross to the right again below a spring. Follow the narrow, overgrown, uphill path alongside a wall, then zig-zag left and right, and continue until you come to the beginning of a narrow kalderimi. **Note that this stretch can become very overgrown with brambles, and the time you take will depend on how difficult the path is when you tackle it. Therefore the next timing should be taken as only a very rough approximation.**

Follow the kalderimi as it winds uphill. It reaches a small level area where it widens slightly into a cart-track and continues to climb until it comes to a T-junction *[10. 21.70'/18.71', 5.49km/370m, approx 30 min].*

Turn right on to the track and walk along to the next T-junction *[11. 21.78'/18.61', 5.69km/200m, 5 min].* Turn right again and go downhill until you meet the tarmac road from Sikaminia to the Skala *[12. 22.05'/18.28', 6.61km/920m, 10 min].* Turn right yet again and walk down the road back to Skala Sikaminias, keeping left at the junction above the village where the road to the right leads to Kagia. Keep on the road until it brings you back to your starting point at the harbour *[13. 22.42'/18.19', 7.78km/1.17km, 15 min].*

World's End – A Circular Walk around Palios

26

Total distance 3 kilometres

Walking time 1 hour

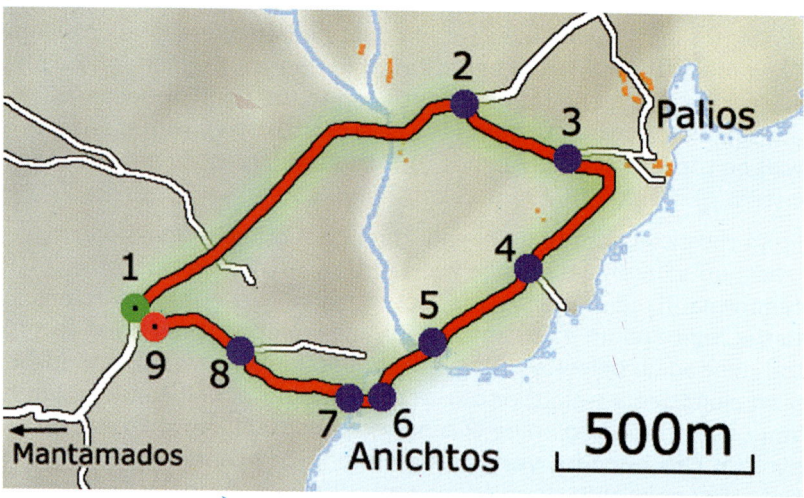

This is a short but varied route through a beautiful and almost untouched part of Lesvos, very different from almost anywhere else on the island. It includes ancient, medieval and modern historical sites, the chance to spot a rare species of duck, a wade across a tidal creek and the opportunity for a swim from a deserted beach, all in an easy hour's walk.

The tiny fishing settlement of Palios (Παλιός) has been described as being at 'the end of the world'. It is isolated on the north-east coast of the island in an idyllic setting at the end of 5½ kilometres of unpaved road, surrounded by largely uncultivated heathland rich in wild heather, lavender, and pine woods, dotted with ponds formed from the disused clay pits which once provided local potters with their raw material. There are still several traditional potteries nearby at Ag Stephanos (Αγ Στέφανος) supplying part-finished ware to the ceramic workshops of Mantamados.

Its few houses and tiny harbour, sheltered by the off-shore Tomaro or Tokmakia islands (Τομαρονήσια ή Τοκμάκια) can seem almost completely cut off from civilisation (even the OTE phone kiosk that used to be here has now disappeared). Yet until less than a century ago there was a thriving port nearby at Anichtos (Ανοιχτός), bringing pilgrims from Asia Minor to worship at the shrine of the Archangel Michael (Archangel – Ταξιάρχης) at Mantamados. In classical Greek and Roman times, through to the end of the Byzantine era, there was a large city here (Παλιός means 'old' or 'ancient'): our walk passes an extensive burial ground with tombs cut from the solid rock, and a much later medieval castle built to protect the area against raids from the sea, but despite this many inhabitants of this and other coastal settlements later moved inland to Mantamados for increased security.

The easiest way to reach the start of this walk is from the Mitilini to Mantamados main road. Take the turning to Aspropotamos (Ασπροπόταμος) about 6km south of Mantamados and follow the asphalt road along the coast for 3½km until it turns inland uphill and reaches a junction where the asphalt continues to the right (signposted Αγ Στέφανος) and a dirt road leads ahead (Παλιός & Λαξευτοί Τάφοι). Take the dirt road; where it divides after 250m turn right, and continue for another 3½km until you come to a track on the right signposted to Ανοιχτός (Anichtos). Park here: this is the starting point of your walk.

Continue along the dirt road from the junction
[1. 39°19.44'/26°24.28']. You will soon pass a large pond on the
right, one of the many disused clay pits in the area, which is a
breeding site for the rare and protected Ruddy Shelduck (*Tadorna
ferruginea*), and which is also home to terrapins and dragonflies.
The large green sign here makes it clear to trigger-happy locals that
shelduck-hunting is forbidden! ('ΚΑΣΤΑΝΟΧΗΝΑ' is its Greek name,
meaning 'Chestnut Goose'). The road runs through a dip, with a
range of rocky crags away to the left, and then comes to a junction
[2. 19.72'/24.83', 1.03km, 15 min].

Turn right, following the sign to ΠΑΛΙΟΣ ΛΙΜΑΝΙ (Palios Harbour).
Just before you reach the hamlet there is a track leading off to the
right *[3. 19.64'/25.07', 1.43km/400m, 5 min]*. Go on to explore
Palios and its harbour and return to this junction when you are
ready. (Measurements continue from here, and exclude your visits
to the village and the rock tombs.)

Go along the side track until you reach a cottage on the right
[4. 19.51'/24.94', 1.76km/330m, 5 min]. The track opposite leads
down to a small landing stage – the rock tombs are scattered across
the slope on each side of this track.

Continue straight past the cottage on a wide path, which becomes a
narrow rocky one running downhill between stone walls. In a field to
the right at the top of the slope you will see a stone-lined pond.

Follow the path down until it reaches a creek. *[5. 19.41'/24.79', 2.06km/300m, 10 min].* To your left, above the mouth of the creek, there are the remains of the medieval castle. there to protect the old harbour of Anichtos and the low-lying bay ahead against raids from the sea.

Go a few metres to your right, then cross the creek where a line of stones mark a ford: the depth of water will depend on the state of the tide, but is rarely more than shin-deep, and the bottom is usually smooth and firm. Once you reach the other side, walk along the beach until you reach a large rock with a farm building on the slope above. (At the time of writing, there are painted requests on the rock, in Greek and French, not to forget to take your rubbish with you) *[6. 19.34'/24.69', 2.24km/180m, 5 min].*

Take the path immediately before the rock, which leads diagonally up to the farm building. Go round to the right of the building and continue on the rocky path going up to the left behind it. The path emerges on to a small level space, meeting a wide path going ahead and uphill to the right *[7. 19.34'/24.64', 2.33km/90m, 5 min].*

Turn right, and follow the path up to a T-junction with a track *[8. 19.41'/24.45', 2.66km/330m, 5 min].* Turn left, and go along the track, passing a pond on your right, until you reach your starting point at a T-junction with the dirt road *[9. 19.44'/24.28', 2.95km/290m, 5 min].*

To the Waterfall of Man'katsa

27

Total distance 3½ kilometres

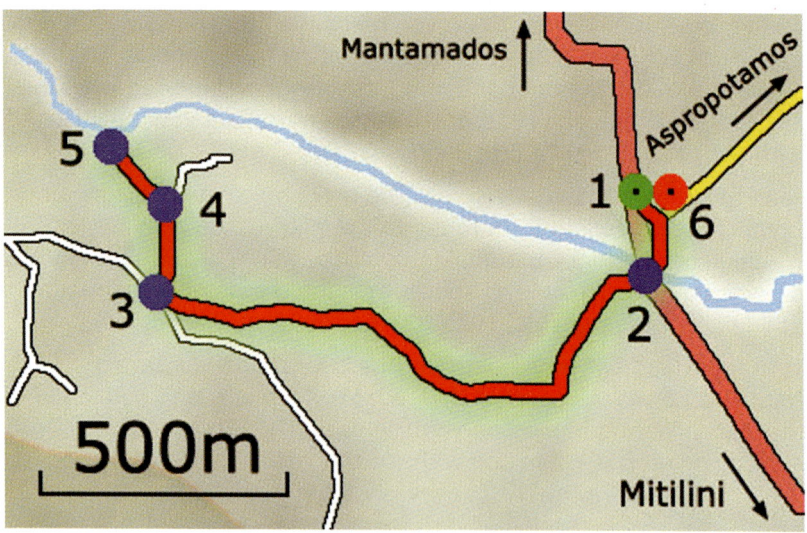

The waterfall of Man'katsa (Μαν'κάτσα) is not only the most impressive, and perhaps the most beautiful on Lesvos, but also the most unexpected, as the deep ravine into which it falls is hidden in a relatively gentle landscape not far from the sea south of Mantamados. It is also the only waterfall on Lesvos with its own (Greek) Facebook page! Even in summer and early autumn, when there is little or no water flowing, it is well worth a visit, and so we have added this short walk, even though our best efforts over several seasons have so far failed to find an acceptable circular route. We suggest that you combine it with the preceding short walk around Palios, which although only a few kilometres away takes you through a strikingly different landscape.

The walk starts and finishes at the junction to Aspropotamos (Ασπροπόταμος) on the main Mitilini – Mantamados road, about 6km south of Mantamados. Park off the road on the open space behind the bus shelter.

From the parking space *[1. 39°16.53'/26°22.31']* cross the Aspropotamos road and take the track across the old stone bridge opposite. Cross the main road, and turn right onto the track a few metres down to the left *[2. 16.47'/22.32', 150m, 4 min].*

Go along this track: you pass an ancient two-arched stone bridge carrying a kalderimi on your left, and then walk alongside a rocky stream, also on your left. Pass the end of a concrete track leading away to the left and look out for a gated track about fifty metres further on the right (there may be a sign on the gate, in English, advertising 'Lesvos Adventure') *[3. 16.45'/21.64', 1.31km/1.16km, 15 min].*

Walk up the track until it divides, and then take the path off to the left (the track itself veers right and ends at a gated olive grove) *[4. 16.55'/21.64', 1.49km/180m, 3 min].* The path is well-defined and signed (to Μαν'κάτσα) as it wanders through wild olive and holly-oak trees until it reaches a picnic table in a small open area. *[5. 16.60'/21.57', 1.65km/160m, 3 min].*

Directly ahead of you is the edge of the ravine, with excellent views of the waterfall over to your left. If you follow the cliff edge for a few metres round to the left you will see a path leading down through the trees. It continues down on steps to the foot of the falls, and also allows you to explore the beautiful stream which flows away from the falls through rock pools down the valley towards the sea.

Returning to the top of the cliff and going further round to the right brings you to the top of the 'flying fox' rope slide, from where you will see the multi-coloured algae on the cliffs to the right of the ravine. If your visit happens to coincide with one of Lesvos Adventure's groups, you may also see the flying fox in action, as well as rock-climbing and abseiling. Who knows, you may even decide to sign up yourselves!

Afterwards, complete your walk by retracing the outward route to the main road, and across to your vehicle *[6. 16.53'/22.31', 3.30km/1.65km, 25 min]*.